PRAGUE
PRAGUE
PRAGUE
PRAGUE
PRAGUE

JIŘÍ HRŮZA
BLAHOMÍR BOROVIČKA

PRAGUE

A SOCIALIST CITY

ORBIS
PRESS AGENCY
PRAGUE 1985

CONTENTS:

Rich history, wealth of architectural monuments and its social and cultural life make Prague, the capital of the Czechoslovak Socialist Republic, a city of great significance in the world. It is Czechoslovakia's only city with over a million inhabitants and one of the most important industrial centres. Prague is the seat of supreme state, scientific, educational, medical and cultural institutions.

The development of Prague as the capital of an advanced socialist country proceeds from historical values and traditions which should be retained for future generations and enriched by new works of the socialist era. An awareness of the significance of this heritage makes it possible to blend new construction with inherited values.

This book traces the history of Prague's urban development, including the projects carried out over the past forty years since the end of World War II. It also outlines the present-day state of the city, its development aims and intended transformations in the coming decades.

Prague is not only an interesting →
historical town but also a major
contemporary metropolis. It is
surrounded by large residential
districts, parks and industrial areas.

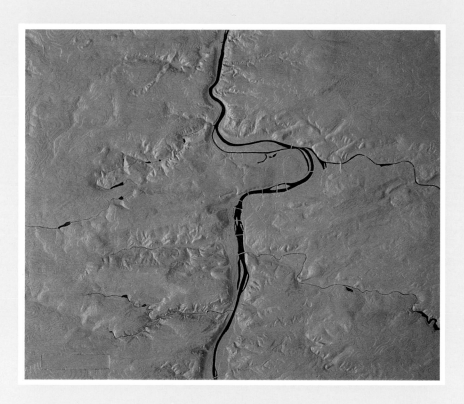

*The river Vltava carves up
a variegated terrain in Prague, with
differences in altitude up to 200
metres.*

Natural conditions have always played a significant role in Prague's development. The river, the varied terrain as well as preserved green belts have helped to shape the unique picture of the city and enrich its environment. On the other hand, especially the varied terrain with great differences in altitude tends to increase the costs of building transport routes and public utilities as many bridges and tunnels have to be constructed.

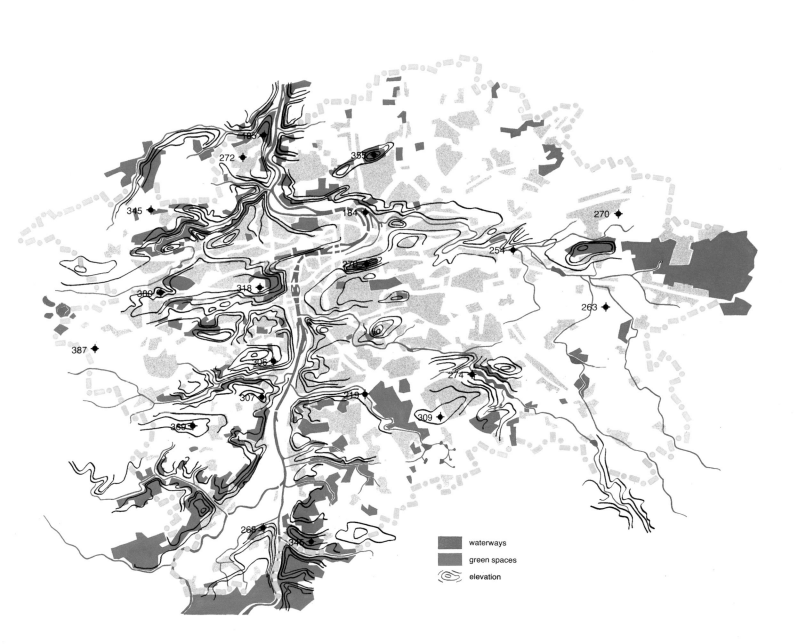

waterways

green spaces

elevation

Prague's historical centre was shaped between the 10th and 14th centuries. Four independent royal towns grew up between the two castles situated on both sides of the river. In the year 1784 the four boroughs merged into one administrative unit. From the 14th century up to the mid-19th century the territory within the Gothic ramparts and later on baroque fortifications was sufficient for the development of Prague. New suburbs mushroomed from the mid-19th century onwards.

castles

settlements up to the early 13th century

Havel Town, founded after 1230

Old Town ramparts, after 1230

Lesser Quarter, founded in 1257

Hradčany, founded after 1320

New Town, founded in 1348

new ramparts in 1348

the town's development within new ramparts

fortifications circa 1650

HISTORY

Prague is one of the most admirable historical towns both as regards the size of its medieval centre and the wealth and significance of its cultural and architectural monuments.

Its geographic position in the heart of the Bohemian Basin in a spot ideally suited for crossing the river Vltava, which flows most of its way through deep valleys, was one of the reasons for the establishment of early human settlements in the area. Archaeological excavations provide ample evidence that in the era of Central European prehistoric cultures the area of present-day Prague was a major settlement and a centre of production and long-distance trade. Hunters of the Bronze Age used to roam the region, while archaeological finds from the Iron Age point to the existence of densely populated settlements, burgeoning crafts and thriving trade.

The foundation of Prague coincides with the arrival of Slavonic tribes which set up agricultural settlements and, beginning in the 8th century A.D., strongholds perched on hills overlooking the Vltava river and its tributaries. In the early stages, the territory of Bohemia and Prague belonged to the sphere of influence of the Slavonic Great Moravia. In the latter half of the 9th century the seat of Přemyslid princes was transferred from the northern periphery of what is today Prague to the area of Prague Castle around which—as archaeological finds tell us—ancient human settlements were known to exist. Prague became the centre of the Czech tribe which gradually came to dominate the entire territory of what is Bohemia and Moravia today. Prague's second castle, Vyšehrad, which in the 11th and 12th centuries for a time vied for power with Prague Castle, was built in the 10th century.

From the 10th to the 12th century an extensive settlement grew up between the two castles, notably on the hilltops and near fords. In the 12th century this settlement had already assumed the character of a town with its stone ecclesiastical and secular buildings, workshops and market-places. The centre of the town shaped itself around what is the present-day Old Town Square. In the middle of the 12th century, the town's ancient wooden bridge was replaced by the Romanesque Judith Bridge, made of stone, which connected the castles and settlements on both river banks.

The hill on which Prague Castle stands was among the earliest inhabited areas in Prague. Archaeological finds assert that in its vicinity a Slavonic settlement existed in the 9th century. Some archaeologists put the foundation of Prague Castle to the last quarter of the 9th century, other scientists claim a yet older settlement existed on its site.

16

In the 11th and 12th centuries Vyšehrad, founded on a rocky headland over the Vltava river, vied for power with Prague Castle. According to ancient legends Vyšehrad is older than Prague Castle but archaeological finds as well as written records indicate that it was built in the 10th century.

The first third of the 13th century marked a very important period in Prague's medieval development. That was the time of the establishment of the first new town near Havel (or St. Gill) market-place, founded as an extension of the existing Old Town. Shortly afterwards, the Old Town proper incorporating the new Havel Town was delineated by ramparts, along with the ancient Jewish Town which had retained its autonomy. In the year 1257 Prague grew a step further with the foundation and fortification of the present-day Lesser Town, situated on the left bank between the Castle and the stone bridge. This new town, which spread along the line connecting the bridge with the Castle, had its centre in a spacious rectangular market-place, the present Lesser Town Square. In the first third of the 14th century, Hradčany, most probably originating as an ancient settlement lying on the castle headland close to major routes leading to the sovereign's seat, was granted municipal rights and privileges.

The medieval development of Prague culminated with the foundation of the New Town by Charles IV in 1348. This was a project unparalleled in contemporary Europe, both in terms of the concept of its layout, scope, impressiveness and breadth of streets and the size of its market-places, nowadays known as Charles, Wenceslas and Gorky Squares.

At the time, the entire territory of the four Prague towns was encircled by new ramparts, which doubled its size and covered a total area of more than 800 hectares (2,000 acres) and was populated by an estimated 50,000 people. Prague was the first medieval metropolis in Central Europe to have its own university, it had its archbishopric, impressive Charles Bridge and a colossal Gothic cathedral began to be built within the castle.

In the early 15th century Prague was one of the centres of the revolutionary Hussite movement, striving for social and church reform of the medieval society and church. The town's significant position was corroborated by the fact that in 1458 George of Poděbrady was elected the King of Bohemia in the town hall of Prague. Monuments of the Hussite tradition have survived in such memorable buildings as the Bethlehem Chapel where Jan Hus (John Huss) delivered his sermons or Vítkov Hill, the site of the defeat of the Crusaders by the Hussite army commanded by Jan Žižka of Trocnov.

Prague's Old Town was founded in the first half of the 13th century by the walling in of an earlier Romanesque settlement which stretched for several miles along the right river bank. The Old Town Square was a centre of the township already at that time. Most of the streets which were built on the sites of ancient lanes in the 11th and 12h centuries have survived in their original form to this day.

↑ Prague prides itself on many Romanesque buildings. Apart from many churches, there are remnants of some 50 Romanesque houses and courtyards, especially in the Old Town. One of the highlights of Prague's Romanesque architecture is the the early 10th century St. George's Church at Prague Castle to which a monastery was added later on. The church today houses collections of the National Art Gallery.

↑ Gothic architecture had dominating influence on the construction of the centre of Prague. Its ground plan, including four historical towns and their ramparts which outlined the historical centre for the following five centuries, was laid out in the Gothic period. One of the best examples of Gothic architecture is St. Vitus' Cathedral at Prague Castle. Its Golden Gate was decorated by a unique mosaic "The Last Judgement" in the latter half of the 14th century.

The Renaissance period has not left behind so many architectural monuments as the preceding Gothic or the subsequent baroque period. Still Prague has a fair sample of Renaissance architectural monuments, including the Summer House of Bohemian Queens with an adjoining garden decorated with the "Singing Fountain". This was built in the mid-16th century and is generally regarded as the most exquisite and stylistically purest Renaissance structure outside Italy.

The 16th century saw an architectural upsurge of Prague as a residence of kings and emperors, priding itself on many outstanding works of Renaissance art. Noblemen's resistance to the Habsburg dynasty which had seized the Czech throne culminated in the unfortunate Battle of White Mountain in 1620. This led to anti-reformation, recatholicization and loss of independence for the Kingdom of Bohemia. During the Thirty Years' War the population of Prague dwindled, including Czech aristocracy and intelligentsia. The town's riches and numerous art treasures were ransacked and carried away by occupying armies.

Newly rich aristocrats and countless ecclesiastical institutions settled in Prague, finding in its baroque architecture and fine arts an ideological instrument to express their power ambitions. The imperial court was transferred to Vienna but Prague still remained the capital city of the Kingdom of Bohemia, its strategic position enhanced by powerful fortifications. A period of economic recovery gradually set in and the town regained its one-time position of a major European cultural and arts centre. At the same time, the first signs of the Czech national revival appeared in the form of vigorous opposition to forced Germanization.

By the end of the 18th century, Prague was greatly affected by the reforms of Emperor Joseph II who abolished many antiquated church institutions and in 1784 ordered a merger of Prague's four historical towns and their councils under the jurisdiction of a single bureaucratic magistrate. That was also the time of the foundation of the first manufacturing workshops and emerging suburbs beyond the city ramparts. In 1817 the suburb of Karlín was founded in a planned fashion and other suburban districts such as Smíchov, Libeň, Vinohrady, Žižkov, Nusle and Holešovice-Bubny followed suit within the next half a century. Large-scale industry mushroomed in these districts which gradually achieved the status of independent towns and at the end of the century they were inhabited by two thirds of Prague's total population of more than half a million. It was at that time that the working class appeared on Prague's historical scene, most of the workers being employed in textile and engineering factories.

In the middle of the 19th century, the Jewish Town was administratively incorporated into Prague, later on followed by Vyšehrad. Up to the year 1866, Prague was

The baroque style which appeared in Prague in the early 17th century was so widespread that newly built baroque structures and particularly baroque reconstructions of older objects substantially affected the overall architectural character of the historical centre. One of the earliest baroque buildings was the sumptuous Wallenstein Palace, surrounded by a garden. More than 20 older houses had to be pulled down to give way to the palace.

In the 17th and 18th centuries many exquisite gardens were laid out in Prague. A real gem among these is the small but charming Vrtba Garden, adorned with sculptures by Mathyas Braun.

Like many other European cities, in the late 19th century Prague succumbed to the "fashion" of urban renewal or slum clearance. One of the victims was the Jewish Town of which only synagogues, a town-hall and an ancient cemetery remain. Pařížská (Paris) Street is the main thoroughfare of the district.

←— In the middle of the 19th century Prague underwent far-reaching changes. The free-flowing Vltava river was lined by newly built embankments, out of which the Smetana Embankment has retained its classicist appearance. It was there that the National Theatre, indisputably the most beautiful neo-Renaissance building in Prague, was built following nation-wide fund-raising campaigns.

Many interesting architectural landmarks were built in Prague in the period between the two world wars. A small "town" of film studios, a quarter of villas and a restaurant with an observation tower and terraces were built in the southern outskirts of Prague. The whole district was named Barrandov after the French geologist who carried out research in the Bohemian Karst region in 19th century.

Prague is justifiably known as a major centre of modern architecture, its 20th century architectural monuments being protected and maintained as carefully as works of art from earlier centuries. One of the gems of 20th century architecture is this building from the late 1930's, today the headquarters of Czechoslovakia's Revolutionary Trade Union Movement.

← By the end of the 19th century extensive exhibitions grounds, including spacious steel halls for the exhibition of industrial products, were built in Prague. At present the area is known as Julius Fučík Park of Culture and Recreation where fairs, sports events and exhibitions are held.

The Soviet Army liberated Prague on May 9th 1945. Thanks to its swift military operation Prague was saved from destruction in the last days of World War II. One section of Prague's Olšany cemetery is the burial ground of Soviet soldiers killed in action in Prague at the end of the Second World War.

← *One of the highlights of contemporary architecture is the building of the Motokov foreign trade corporation in the southern part of Prague.*

a fortified town and it was not until 1874 that the ramparts began to be pulled down. In 1884 the districts of Holešovice-Bubny and later Libeň were joined to Prague which thus covered an area of 2,100 hectares and by the end of the 19th century had a population in excess of 200,000 people, the suburbs not included. By that time the Habsburg monarchy was no longer capable of holding up the town's development and the mounting Czech nationalist movement which found its expression in the grandiose construction of the National Theatre.

After the end of the First World War and the proclamation of the independent Czechoslovak Republic in 1918, Prague became the capital city and the seat of the government. In 1920, as many as 37 outlying communities were attached to Greater Prague and the city's overall area grew to more than 17,000 hectares. Its population swelled to 670,000 and by the late 1930's it approached the one million mark. New public buildings, banking and other financial institutions and industrial enterprises sprang up in Prague, a genuine show case of modern architecture. In spite of vigorous housing construction the city's acute housing shortage remained unresolved and shanty towns mushroomed in the suburban areas. Prague grew to be a typical capitalist city with all its contradictions and bitter class struggles in which the working class was led by the Communist Party of Czechoslovakia.

The Munich betrayal, occupation by Nazi Germany and the outbreak of World War II brought the country and its people untold suffering, human, material and cultural losses. During the war, Prague was also a major centre of anti-fascist resistance, withstanding Nazi brutality as well as savage attempts at Germanization.

The country's liberation by the Soviet Army and the uprising of the Czech people against the Nazis in 1945 ushered in a new era of socialist construction. The 1950's saw the implementation of the first ambitious comprehensive plans, the first housing estates and Prague's most significant architectural monuments restored to their one-time beauty. This trend continued well into the 1960's when more than one million inhabitants lived in Prague, then a city spreading over some 300 square kilometres. Snowballing traffic problems which could not be tackled by any other available means led to the decision to build the Metro, an underground railway system, in Prague.

In the 1970's, the volume of investment in urban development was substantially raised and long-term plans were drawn up, notably the general plan and the master plan. The construction of the Metro got into full swing and new large residential areas—known as the North, South and Southwest Towns were under construction. Work began on Prague's basic communication system, its public utility services were improved and special attention was focused on environmental protection. After the incorporation of another thirty villages in 1974, the territory of Greater Prague grew by an additional 200 square kilometres, totalling some 500 square kilometres. According to the 1980 census the Czechoslovak capital had a population of almost 1.2 million. At the instigation of the Czechoslovak government, planners from Prague and the Central Bohemian Region devised an urban development plan of the Prague conurbation, which covers more than 3,700 square kilometres. The plan serves predominantly to streamline civil engineering projects in Prague and its adjacent territory. At present the city is entering a new period in keeping with the attained level of the development of society, its requirements and possibilities.

← *The southern front of the Old Town Hall is formed by a unique grouping of objects built from 1338 onwards. In the last days of World War II the building was extensively damaged. At present the Old Town Hall is the seat of the Municipal National Committee (City council) in Prague.*

THE PRESENT

Prague is the capital city of the federative Czechoslovak Socialist Republic as well as the capital of the Czech Socialist Republic. As regards to its administrative status, Prague is on a par with any of the ten regions which make up the whole of Czechoslovakia. Prague is the seat of the administrative bodies of the Central Bohemian Region and is run by the elected National Committee (city council). Each of the municipal districts into which the city is divided has its own District National Committee. Larger communities and settlements which have been incorporated into Prague since the end of World War II have retained their own Local National Committees.

Present-day Prague betrays all the traces of historical development over the past eleven centuries. At the same time the city is greatly affected by prevailing natural conditions particularly the geological relief, with differences in altitude of more than 200 metres. The backbone of Prague is the Vltava river which flows from south to north. Along with a number of tributaries, rivulets and streams, the Vltava has carved a variegated terrain with deep valleys, hills and elevated terraces on which new development is mostly concentrated.

Historical and natural conditions were instrumental in dividing the city into several typical zones which differ in terms of origin, conception and architecture.

The historical centre, situated in the Vltava valley, forms the heart of the city. In its structure the original four historical towns and two castles are still discernible. On the right bank is the Old Town, New Town, and Vyšehrad, while the Lesser Town, Hradčany and the dominating Prague Castle are situated on the left. Some remnants od medieval ramparts as well as mid-17th century baroque fortifications have been preserved particularly on the left bank of the Vltava.

In 1971, the Czechoslovak government proclaimed the entire historical centre, covering an area of almost 900 hectares, an urban reservation protected by law. As many as thirteen national cultural monuments are to be found in its territory, including Prague Castle, Vyšehrad and Charles Bridge, as well as more than 1,400 protected architectural monuments, such as 105 palaces, 35 monasteries and convents, 58 churches, 10 chapels, historical gardens and scores of burghers' houses. Out of the total of roughly 10,000 protected works of art and

*In the 19th and especially 20th century Prague underwent
a period of fast development. In the early 20th century two
suburbs were joined to Prague. In 1900 the town had twice as
many inhabitants as the original historical centre. Greater
Prague came into existence in 1922 following the addition of
surrounding villages. Half a century later Prague's territory grew
to almost 500 square kilometres, providing sufficient scope for
development.*

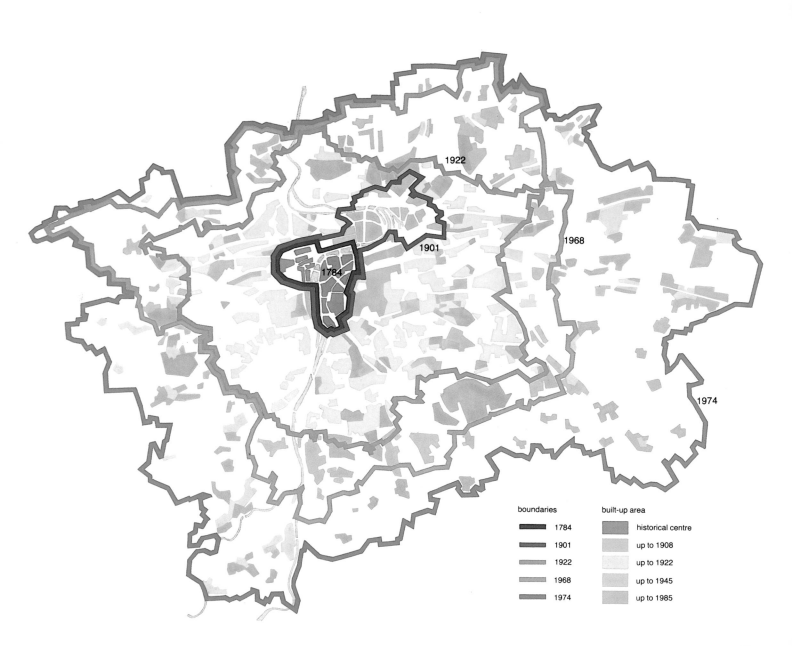

boundaries	built-up area
1784	historical centre
1901	up to 1908
1922	up to 1922
1968	up to 1945
1974	up to 1985

32

In terms of urban development, the city is divided into four concentric zones. The first of these is the historical centre surrounded by the inner city, formed by the original suburbs from the late 19th and early 20th centuries. Most of the modern housing construction since 1945 has been concentrated in the outer city. The fourth zone, situated in the city's outer perimeter, is mostly made up of agricultural land.

historical centre
inner city
urbanized area
administrative boundary

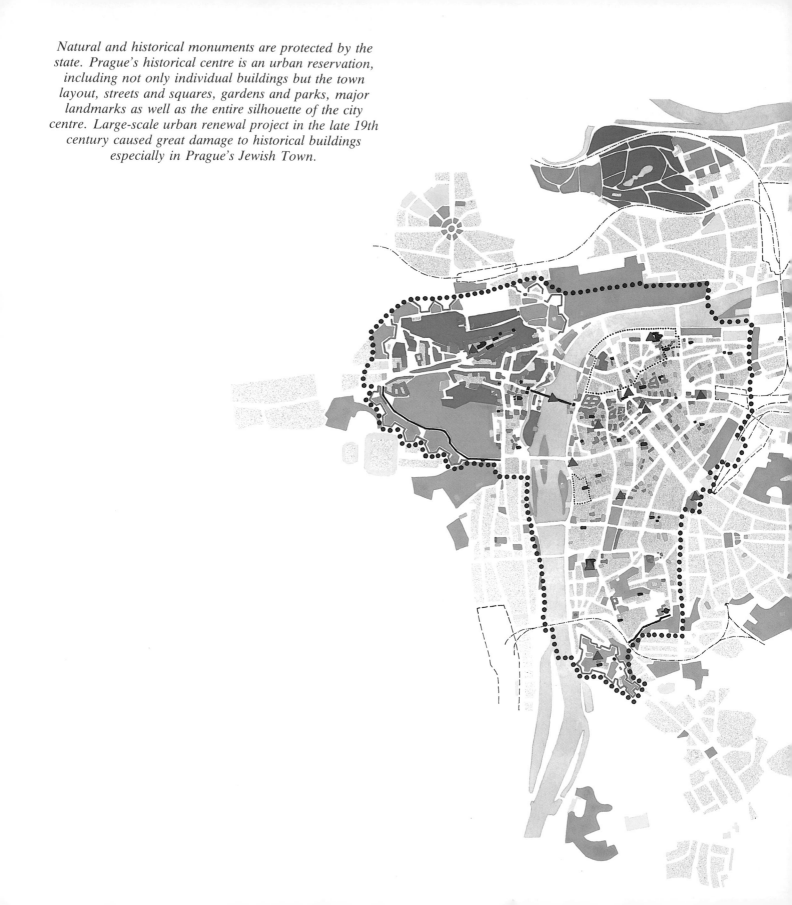

Natural and historical monuments are protected by the state. Prague's historical centre is an urban reservation, including not only individual buildings but the town layout, streets and squares, gardens and parks, major landmarks as well as the entire silhouette of the city centre. Large-scale urban renewal project in the late 19th century caused great damage to historical buildings especially in Prague's Jewish Town.

▲   national cultural monuments

▇   Romanesque and Gothic

▇   Renaissance and baroque

▇   19th century

▢   20th century

●●●●   boundary of Prague's urban reservation

⋯⋯   renewal districts

▇   historical gardens up to the late 18th century

▇   19th and 20th century parks

artifacts most are registered in the territory of Prague's historical centre.

The original silhouette of the city, formed by countless steeples, spires and towers, which have given it the name of the city of a hundred spires, has survived up to this day. Great efforts have been made to preserve the original lay-out of squares and streets, documenting their development over the centuries and attesting to their unique value. Considerable care has been devoted to the protection and maintenance of these monuments, especially since 1945.

Prague's historical centre accounts for mere 1.6 per cent of the city's total administrative area; it is inhabited by some 70,000 people, roughly 6 per cent of the overall population, and offers almost 200,000 job opportunities, which represent one third of all jobs in Prague.

The second zone encircling the historical centre is called the inner city. This is formed by the former sprawling suburbs that grew up from the mid-19th to the mid-20th centuries. The street pattern and architecture of the inner city survives as evidence documenting the time of its origin. This zone is a mixture of industrial and residential areas, its territory is densely built up and its public utilities, transport facilities and technical installations no longer comply with current requirements. Naturally, there is still a great difference between former working class and bourgeois districts. The inner city, too, prides itself on many architectural monuments. Indeed, the entire inner city is a protected zone of the Prague Urban Reservation.

The inner city covers an area almost 10 times bigger than the historical centre. It occupies some 7,500 hectares on which 600,000 inhabitants, approximately half of the entire population, live. At the beginning of this century, there were some 200,000 people more living in the area but at the cost of heavy overcrowding. In Žižkov, for example, the population density was more than 1,000 inhabitants per a hectare of residential area. The inner city also provides over 300,000 job opportunities, some 45 per cent of the Prague total. It is in the inner city that Prague faces the most acute environmental problems due to its combination of industrial and residential areas, mostly surviving from the 19th century, all this being aggravated by exceptionally dense traffic.

Prague is often called a city of a hundred spires. Particularly the city centre boasts of dozens of Gothic, baroque and other spires, steeples and towers.

The Lesser Town on the left bank →
of the river Vltava is one of Prague's most picturesque districts. It was founded in the year 1257 as the second Prague town. Most of its buildings are baroque reconstructions of former Gothic or Renaissance objects.

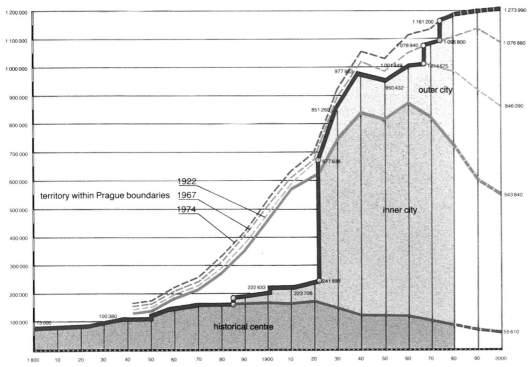

Wenceslas Square was laid out in the middle of the 14th century as a medieval market-place. Nowadays it is a major commercial centre, lined with hotels, pedestrian zones and green spaces.

The city's population growth also attests to the changes Prague has undergone, reflecting not only the gradual extension of municipal boundaries but also a decrease in overcrowding in the historical centre and inner city. More and more inhabitants are moving to the city's outer development zone where soon one half of the population will be living.

Most of Prague's housing stock that is due for modernization is concentrated in the inner city. A basic prerequisite for this, however, is reconstruction of antiquated public utility networks. The road network, dating back to the late 19th century, also falls short of the current requirements of public transport. Some parts of the inner city suffer from a severe shortage of parking and recreation facilities. That is why particular care is dedicated to trees and open spaces. Inhabitants of these districts themselves give a helping hand in the establishment and upkeep of small parks and children's playgrounds.

Those parts of the inner city, situated alongside the main thoroughfares and arteries, fulfill a special role as social centres, concentrating important cultural, educational, scientific and other institutions which cannot be located in the historical centre. Being part and parcel of the historical centre, they form community centres that belong to outer districts. The importance of these areas is further enhanced by the Metro stations which, as a rule, constitute unique architectural landmarks.

The third area, built almost exclusively in the latter half of the 20th century, is the outer city, also designated "a development zone". Twice as large as the historical centre and the inner city put together, it is inhabited by almost half a million people who live in flats mostly built after 1945. Before the war, small communities and settlements, most of them founded in the Middle Ages, used to stand here. In addition to communal and cooperative-based housing construction, this area is noted for many family houses, with the municipal authorities providing services and building roads.

New work places are being created in Prague's outer development zone. Most of these are concentrated in the industrial districts of Malešice and Hostivař, founded in the eastern outskirts in the early 1950's. Smaller industrial areas are established in the vicinity of new residential districts. Social centres in the outer zone house diverse cultural, administrative and other institutions which supplement the offer of employment opportunities, making Prague's new quarters still more attractive to live in. In all, the outer city offers as many as 200,000 jobs. However, some parts, especially the southern outskirts, are mainly residential and local inhabitants have to commute to work, predominantly to the city centre.

← The Vltava river in Prague is spanned by 15 bridges.

← *This aerial view shows not only the beautiful layout of the Lesser Town with Prague Castle towering above it but also a panorama of the northern parts of the city built in the 19th and 20th centuries.*

Prague's urbanistic composition features three main highlights: the historical centre, residential districts built between the two world wars and the North Town built in the 1960's.

The district of Smíchov, situated on the left bank of the river, was built in the second half of the 19th century. Originally an industrial quarter, it is now predominantly a residential district offering stunning views of the ancient Vyšehrad Castle or the modern Palace of Culture.

A significant feature of the outer zone are its parks, sports and recreation centres. The parks are mostly laid out in the shape of wedges, pointing from the suburbs towards the city centre. These include open spaces along the Vltava river, undeveloped slopes as well as former enclosures and gardens adjoining suburban farmsteads, etc. These green belts are of exceptional importance, serving to make the city more varied and beautiful. Many parts of these green zones are protected as nature reserves or geological and archaeological localities.

The fourth belt within Prague's administrative boundaries, is comprised of agricultural land and tracts of countryside, covering approximately 200 square kilometres and accounting for almost 40 per cent of the entire territory of the city. These areas, situated mainly beyond Prague's outer ring-road, are populated by some 20,000 people, mostly inhabitants of smaller communities. This particular zone of Prague is excepted to retain its rural character with prevailing state farms run by the municipal authorities. Furthermore, new parks, orchards, and greenhouses for growing vegetables are to be laid out there.

The ultimate aim is to upgrade the suburban landscape in order to preserve its numerous natural beauty spots. A total of 53 protected nature reserves, spreading over an area of almost 1,500 hectares, is to be found in the territory of Czechoslovakia's capital, while another 40 smaller tracts with a total area of 200 hectares are to be added in the future. All in all, some 3.4 per cent of the territory of Prague will thus be formed by nature reserves.

The picture of the city would be incomplete without mentioning the conurbation of which Prague is the centre. Prague included, the conurbation occupies an area of about 3,700 square kilometres and the number of inhabitants is around the 1.7 million mark. The density of population in this territory is 450 inhabitants per a square kilometre, while in the city proper there are 24,000 inhabitants per square kilometre. The conurbation takes up approximately one third of the area of the Central Bohemian administrative region. As to planning measures concerning the conurbation and the capital city, they are approved by the government of the Czech Socialist Republic. At the instigation of the Czech government, the Prague Municipal National

In the year 1420 the Czech Hussite →
*army defeated a much stronger
enemy, the Crusaders, on Vítkov
Hill in Prague. The National
Memorial, built in the 1930's,
commemorates the revolutionary
traditions of the Czech people.*

One of priorities in the urban →
*development of Czechoslovakia's
capital is reconstruction of
suburban areas. Entering Prague
from the east, visitors pass
a modern training centre for
building workers, complete with
indoor swimming pool, and a car
sales room with service.*

*The idea to bridge the valley
dividing the historical centre from
Prague's southern terrace was born
in the late 19th century. The
Klement Gottwald Bridge which
spans the valley was opened in
1974, serving both car traffic and
one line of the Prague Metro
leading to the South Town.*

The Prague conurbation covers an area of 1,700 square kilometres and is inhabited by approximately 1.7 million people. Development plans for the city and the Prague conurbation are closely coordinated. Most people living in the suburbs commute to work in the city. A very large number of Prague people spend their weekends in recreation areas situated around the city. The whole territory of the Prague conurbation is linked on to Prague's transport and public utility networks. While recreation areas are to be found mostly in the southern parts of the conurbation, major agricultural and industrial districts, including the industrial towns of Kladno, Kralupy, Neratovice and many others, are situated in its northern reaches.

settlements
green areas
roads
boundaries of Prague
boundaries of conurbations

Committee and the Central Bohemian Regional National Committee set up a Joint Standing Committee to harmonize their town-planning, environmental protection measures and projects.

Prague has a special relationship with the Central Bohemian region and indeed, as the capital city, with the entire country. This applies particularly to cultural, educational, scientific and other institutions of nation-wide importance based in Prague, but also to commuting and services, communications and transport networks, water supplies, etc. With the growth in recreation and tourism, a growing number of visitors come to Prague, attracted by its historical and cultural monuments. On the other hand, many Prague inhabitants leave the city for weekends and holidays. In the summer, many people are known to head for the Vltava dam lakes and the wooded areas south of Prague, while in winter their destination is either the Giant Mountains or the Šumava mountain range.

This was just a brief outline of the face of contemporary Prague which can hardly aspire to depict the wealth and variety of its life, activities etc. It just touched upon the basic characteristics of Prague, a city which has succeeded in combining the beauty of an ancient historical and cultural tradition with present-day social and economic development. It may possibly be instrumental in telling you about the city, its history, present and future.

The contemporary face of the city is depicted in this map showing industrial and residential areas, public amenities, green spaces, sports grounds, transport routes and public utilities. Clearly discernible is the historical centre and inner city, surrounded by freely spaced out residential and industrial districts. Agricultural land, including over 50 communities attached to Prague in the 1960's and 1970's, accounts for almost 40 per cent of the city's territory.

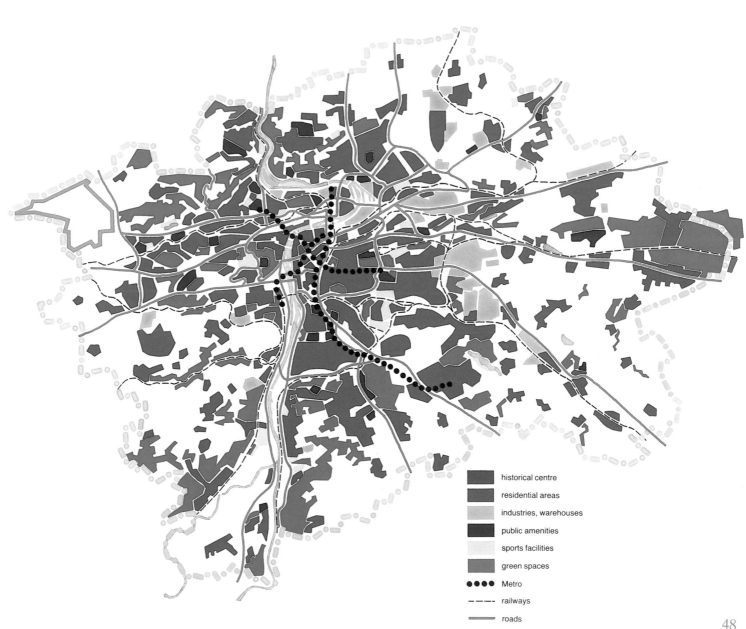

historical centre

residential areas

industries, warehouses

public amenities

sports facilities

green spaces

●●●● Metro

- - - railways

—— roads

DEVELOPMENT

As in any other city, in Prague too, buildings, communications and technical installations were created by past generations to make their own life and that of future generations easier. This is particularly true of housing, industry, culture, health care, administration, transport, water and energy supplies and last but not least recreation and sports.

The development of human settlements in Prague features many specific aspects, determined by historical, present-day and perspective objectives. Prague was founded and developed as an amalgamation of settlements and townships which have over the centuries been harmonized into one urbanistic whole, capable of fulfilling the role of the capital city of an advanced socialist state.

The main trends of the development of Prague are specified in a package of interlinked urban development plans for individual parts of the city. Sites for new residential areas are selected with a view to prevailing natural conditions, existing and perspective work places. Local social and community centres, recreation grounds and lines of public transport are spread evenly throughout the city. Indeed, planning often has to strive for harmonizing contradictory needs and interests. Therefore, Prague's complex social, economic and material fabric is divided into the following subsystems: production and employment, housing, public amenities, open spaces, recreation and sports, transport and services.

Since the mid-19th century engineering has been the main industrial branch in Prague. The city's biggest engineering enterprise is the ČKD works, associating a number of engineering branches, including the manufacture of giant compressors at Vysočany.

ČKD also produces diesel engines →
at Smíchov. After a fire, the plant was reconstructed and modernized.

1. PRODUCTION AND EMPLOYMENT

Prague is not only a much admired architectural jewel but also a major industrial centre offering plenty of jobs in the construction and maintenance of the city, in culture, education, science and research, health care, administration, services, transport, power generation, supplies of raw materials, foodstuffs and many other goods. The city is a great consumer as well as producer of material and spiritual values.

Out of the population of 1.2 million, 635,000 people are of productive age and in addition to them almost 100,000 people, living outside Prague, commute to work in the capital. Prague has a very high rate of employment, almost 54 per cent of all inhabitants, women's employment approaches 50 per cent. The fact that job opportunities outnumber job seekers means that more than 12 per cent of all employed are people past retirement age. Over 63 per cent of all working people are employed in branches of production.

Industry accounts for approximately one quarter of all jobs. As far as individual branches are concerned, almost one half of the jobs are in engineering, with food-processing, electronics and chemical production trailing behind. The second largest group of jobs in Prague is commerce in which more than 15 per cent of all inhabitants are employed. Third is the building industry with 12 per cent, followed by education and culture and administration with 9 per cent each. Transport and communications employ almost 8 per cent of Prague inhabitants, while more than 5 per cent each are employed in science and research and health services and social care.

In the past, employment in Prague was associated with the city's administrative and cultural role and its position as a major transport and commercial centre. The first, predominantly textile manufactures appeared in Prague at the end of the 18th century. In the middle of the 19th century, engineering already established itself as the single most important industrial branch. The first factories were established in the centre of Prague but in the following years manufacturers went out of their way to find more suitable sites in the suburbs, situated by the river and newly built railways. These tracts were usually larger and cheaper and in no time working class residential areas sprang up in their vicinity.

*Industrial districts are mostly situated in the suburbs. Most
employment opportunities, however, are offered in the inner city
where social and cultural institutions and services are
concentrated. According to town-planning intentions, it is
desirable to maintain the residential character of the city centre.
On the other had, new job opportunities should be created in
the vicinity of modern residential quarters, particularly in the
southern and southwestern parts of Prague.*

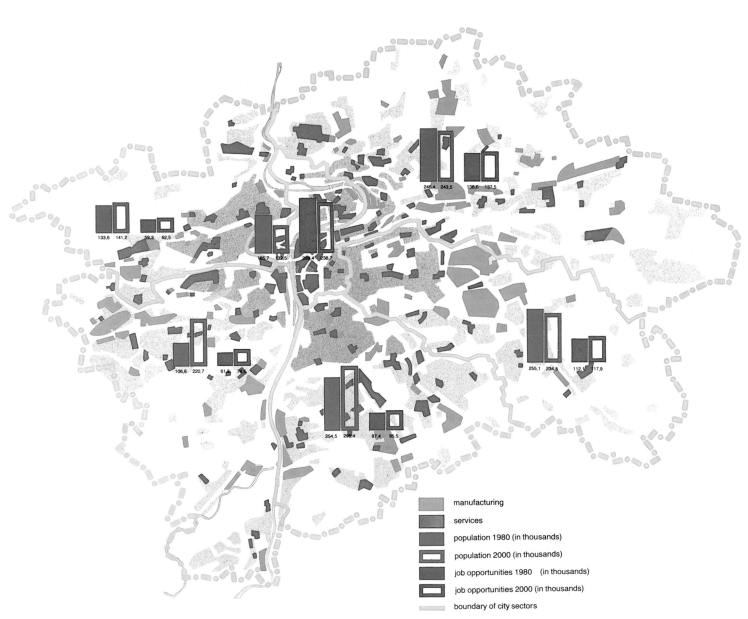

	manufacturing
	services
	population 1980 (in thousands)
	population 2000 (in thousands)
	job opportunities 1980 (in thousands)
	job opportunities 2000 (in thousands)
	boundary of city sectors

The planned development of Prague after 1945 and the nationalization of industry made it possible to implement the overall concept of promoting major industrial branches. Since then, the capital has retained its significant role in the country's economic life, while great efforts have been made to improve both the conditions of industrial production and its impact on the town. Modernization and automation are currently the main priorities in Prague's industry, which in turn helps to raise production and save manpower.

Industry in Prague covers almost one half of all production branches in Czechoslovakia, the most important being engineering, electronics and metal-working which account for more than 60 per cent of the city's gross industrial production. Furthermore, Prague is noted for a wide range of other branches, including the light, chemical, printing and food-processing industries as well as designing, and foreign and domestic trade.

Naturally, industrial branches aimed at satisfying consumer needs occupy a place of their own. The city and its industries could hardly function without its own power generation, building industry, manufacture of building materials, road haulage and communications.

In the non-production sphere, Prague enjoys an exclusive position in such branches as science and research, higher education, culture, banking and insurance, tourist services and nationwide social and administrative institutions. The same applies to housing management, social care, public transport, communal services and municipal administration, some of the city's major services.

In the future Prague is expected to retain those industrial branches which have prospects of making the best use of the qualification structure of the working people in Prague, the local science and research establishments as well as the interlinks existing between individual branches. There is an overriding trend towards eliminating production programmes and technologies which adversely affect the living environment, put excessive strain on road haulage and have other negative consequences.

The location of industrial plants in Prague is currently undergoing certain changes too. A completely new industrial area was established in Prague's eastern outskirts after 1950 to accomodate pariculatly factories

Prague is a centre of the pharmaceutical industry, the production of serums and medicaments, laboratory instruments, medical equipment, etc. The Léčiva national enterprise is based in a newly-built plant at Hostivař.

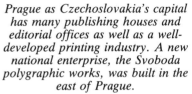

Prague as Czechoslovakia's capital has many publishing houses and editorial offices as well as a well-developed printing industry. A new national enterprise, the Svoboda polygraphic works, was built in the east of Prague.

A new industrial district was founded in the eastern part of Prague in 1950 to accomodate industrial enterprises moved from the city centre. One of these is Ferona dealing in metallurgical products.

54

Electronics and computer technology are currently priority branches. The Aritma enterprise, manufacturing computers is situated in the northwest of Prague, providing jobs for the inhabitants of this mostly residential area.

transferred from unsuitable sites in the city centre and warehouses some of which are still to be found in the inner city. In several other localities in the outskirts of Prague, new large-capacity warehouses are being built or are under consideration. As a rule, these areas are easily accessible by municipal transport; the construction of new railway lines is also a possibility.

Industrial districts are also laid out in the vicinity of large housing estates in an effort to facilitate accessibility between residential and industrial areas. A typical example is Southwest Town in the vicinity of which several industrial enterprises have been erected. At present, construction is underway of a new Tatra tram factory to take over production from mid-19th century Tatra factory in the district of Smíchov, once a major industrial suburb. Since then the district has substantially changed and there are countless reasons for using the site of the factory as a community centre to serve the entire district, inhabited by a quarter of million people.

Another example is provided by the late 19th century slaughterhouse in the district of Holešovice-Bubny, now moved to new premises in the northern and southern outskirts of Prague. The site of the former slaughterhouse is currently used as a complex of market-halls until a new adequate construction project is found.

Sometimes production programmes are changed to suit new conditions, as was the case with a former motorcycle factory in the south of Prague. Original plans had reckoned with the demolition of the plant but it was eventually converted into an electronics factory, offering jobs mainly to women living in the adjacent new housing estates.

A similar approach is known to be applied in the non-production sphere. Excessive concentration of different institutions and enterprises in the historical centre and inner city is regarded as unsuitable and new ones are located in suburban areas. Accordingly, most of Prague's technical universities are situated in the north-west of the city, a complex of technical institutes of Czechoslovakia's Academy of Sciences is under construction in the northern outskirts, while major communication centres are concentrated in the eastern parts of Prague. Czechoslovak Television, for instance, has its headquarters in the south of the city and a new building of Czechoslovak Radio is being built nearby. Naturally,

New factories necessitate the construction of new administrative buildings, accommodation facilities for employees and apprentice training centres.

Large greenhouses are mushrooming around Prague to keep the capital well-supplied with fresh vegetables.

Production of precast panels for housing construction.

some well-established institutions, such as the National Art Gallery and Charles University, are housed in their original buildings in the historical centre.

This planned redistribution of industrial and non-production enterprises has been progressing fairly successfully. In spite of that, Prague—like many other large cities—still grapples with the problem of excessive concentration of institutions and enterprises in its historical centre. This leads to a great deal of commuting and subsequent strains on public transport. Seen in this light, one of the priorities in this field is to further improve accessibility between residential and industrial, shopping and commercial areas and eliminate the negative effects of industrial production.

← *Food consumption in a city with a population of more than one million is fairly high. Two meat-processing plants, one in north and the other in south Prague, were recently put into operation. This is the Písnice plant.*

High-rise blocks blend well with the city's terrain and make way for more green areas. A combination of high-rise blocks and houses was used on the Krč housing estate with almost 4,000 housing units.

2. HOUSING

To provide suitable conditions for housing is one of the chief tasks of the development and reconstruction in the city. This entails virtually all aspects of housing, ranging from flats and their furnishings, public amenities, green spaces and recreation facilities to transport, communications and all services. The quality of the living environment is not determined solely by the available space, technical utilities or public amenities but also by the general layout and architectural design.

The housing stock in Prague comprises roughly 470,000 housing units. An overwhelming majority of Prague inhabitants live in flats which are either state-owned or are the property of housing cooperatives. Some 60,000 households, more than 13 per cent of the total, are in privately owned family houses. The number of family houses in Prague exceeds 44,000 and along with adjoining gardens and other premises they take up 58 per cent of the city's residential areas, i.e. over 60 square kilometres.

Prague's extensive historical centre and suburbs built in the late 19th century substantially affect the overall level of housing. Even though more than a half of inhabited flats in Prague were built in the past 40 years, the average age of Prague houses is over 40 years and almost 12 per cent of them were built before the turn of this century. This also influences the average size of flats which are much smaller in older parts than in modern housing estates. The principal cause for this is that 40 per cent of flats in the historical centre and inner city have only a kitchen and one living room.

Approximately 85 per cent of all flats are designated as belonging to what are known in Czechoslovakia as the first and second category flats. This signifies flats with their own toilets and bathrooms, many of them also having central heating. Partially equipped flats are to be found mostly in the older parts of the city and in smaller communities incorporated into Greater Prague over the past 20 years.

Admittedly, the standards of housing greatly differ in the city's individual zones. Thus, in the historical centre there are almost 30,000 flats of which more than half were built prior to 1900 and a mere 500 flats built after 1945. In spite of a sustained drive to modernize inadequate housing as much as 30 per cent of flats in this zone are not fully equipped. A somewhat better situation

Residential areas take up the biggest portion of Prague's territory. Up to the year 2000 the largest building site in Prague will be the Southwest Town for more than 140,000 inhabitants. In addition to new housing construction, the share of modernization and comprehensive reconstruction of existing flats in the inner city and regeneration of the historical centre will keep on increasing.

renewal of historical centre

reconstruction and modernization

new housing construction 1986 — 2000

new housing construction after the year 2000

family houses after 1985

prevails in the inner city where more than 50 per cent of all Prague flats are concentrated. 75 per cent of them were built before 1945 and flats either without their own bathroom, toilet or both account for 15 per cent of the total.

It is in the outer development belt that the best-quality housing can be found. More than 70 per cent of all flats in this area were built after 1945. Out of the total number of 180,000 households, an absolute majority have their own bathrooms, toilets and central heating and almost half of the flats have three or more rooms. Just a small portion of households in the outer belt are situated in rural communities incorporated into the city during the past decades. It is in these parts of Prague where people, intent on building their own family houses, look for suitable building sites. An average of 1,000 familiy houses are built there every year.

In 1945 Prague had a total of 320,000 housing units, including 41,000 of them, i.e. some 13 per cent, that had been demolished or seriously damaged during the war. As a result of the war and the Nazi occupation, construction virtually ground to a halt. In the first post-war years the top priority in construction was to repair the damages caused by the war. Between 1945 and 1955, a mere 14,000 new flats were built but the volume of housing construction has been steadily rising ever since. This was made possible not only by the nationalization and industrialization of the building industry but also by the introduction of novel technologies, notably precasting and since the end of the 1950's the use of panels to assemble blocks of flats.

Over the past 40 years as many as 240,000 new homes have been built in Prague. Roughly 600,000 people, no less than half of Prague's population, now live in these homes. Nevertheless, the net increase in the housing stock over the past four decades totals just over 150,000 flats because more than 90,000 inadequate flats have either been pulled down or converted for purposes other than housing. Between 1970 and 1980, over 94,000 new homes were built in the Czechoslovak capital, more than 20 per cent of the entire housing stock.

Following the period of reconstruction of war-damaged houses and flats immediately after the war, new housing construction was concentrated in empty sites inside existing residential areas unfinished because of the war. But shortly afterwards this type of housing

Much attention is devoted to green spaces in new housing estates. These are taken care of by specialized services along with local citizens' committees which are elected in individual blocks of flats and which cooperate with deputies from District National Committees (borough councils).

Since 1945 new housing construction has been concentrated in the suburban areas. Up to the 1960's newly built residential areas consisted of housing estates for 10 to 20 thousand people. Owing to the growing number of newly built flats larger residential districts, or towns, began to be built. One of the main housing construction projects in the 1960's was the North Town, housing 100,000 inhabitants. At present finishing touches are being put to another Prague residential district, the South Town.

The Novodvorská housing estate, built in the south of Prague in the 1960's for some 12,000 inhabitants, has a popular open-air swimming pool.

LETŇANY
SEVERNÍ MĚSTO
ČERNÝ MOST
ČERVENÝ VRCH
INVALIDOVNA
PETŘINY
MALEŠICE
ŘEPY
SOLIDARITA
RYBNÍČKY
ZAHRADNÍ MĚSTO
PANKRÁC
SPOŘILOV
JIŽNÍ MĚSTO
NOVODVORSKÁ
KRČ
MODŘANY
LHOTKA

The Ďáblice residential district, built in the mid-1970's for some 26,000 inhabitants, is part of the North Town where 100,000 people live. The housing estate is situated on the southern slopes of Ďáblice Forest.

120,000 people live in the North Town, a residential district set on a high terrace over the Vltava.

The Bohnice housing estate with → a population of 33,000, the biggest component of Prague's North Town, was finished in 1980. This aerial view shows the division of this quarter into three sectors grouped around a social centre.

construction was no longer effective and industrial building methods required much larger sites. Therefore, new housing estates and whole residential districts began to mushroom on the outskirts of the city, mostly in locations which can be reached by public transport and easily connected to the existing public utilities. These housing developments—the very first ones, including the cooperative Solidarita housing estate, followed by Petřiny, Červený vrch and Invalidovna where the erection of new types of houses was tested and some other residential areas—each contained on average between 1,000 and 5,000 flats. These housing estates were built complete with crèches, kindergartens, primary schools, health and shopping centres.

The next stage involved the construction of whole "towns". A preview of this urban development concept was provided by a housing estate in the district of Pankrác. The first modern "town" in the true sense of the term was Severní Město (North Town). This was Prague's biggest building site in the 1960's and gradually four residential districts, each named after the original settlement—Prosek, Ďáblice, Kobylisy and Bohnice— were built to accomodate as many as 100,000 people. Each has its own specific character and its own community centre. The North Town was finished before the construction of the Prague Metro whose one line is to be extended there.

The second town was Jižní Město (South Town) which was started in the 1970's. Its eastern sector for 70,000 inhabitants has already been completed and at present finishing touches are being put to its western sector, housing more than 30,000 people. As its name suggests, the South Town is situated on the southern edge of Prague, close to the Prague-Brno-Bratislava motorway. It is encircled by parks, covering an area of more than 500 hectares, coupled with 100 hectares of newly laid-out open spaces and a 38-hectare reservoir used for water sports and recreation. The South Town is Prague's first suburban housing development to be connected by the Metro.

Jihozápadní Město (Soutwest Town) is the third, designed for a total of 140,000 inhabitants. Like its two predecessors, the Southwest Town spreads on a plateau above the Vltava river. Its radial backbone should be Prague's Metro "B" line. Like the North Town, it is

In addition to communal housing
construction, housing cooperatives,
which are heavily subsidized by the
state, are also involved in the
building of new flats in Prague.
Housing cooperatives own multi-
storey houses in residential districts
as well as one-storey family houses.
Terrace houses, as shown in this
picture from the district of Podolí,
are currently very popular.

The sloping terrain on the left bank
of the Vltava river offers ideal sites
for smaller housing estates. A
typical example is this residential
district in Břevnov, built on the site
of older settlements.

subdivided into several districts in accordance with prevailing natural conditions.

In addition to these towns, Prague has several other housing developments as well as centres of cooperative-based housing and privately owned family houses.

All in all, as many as 150,000 homes are expected to be built or modernized in Prague between 1985 and 2000. These will be built by the city, individual industrial enterprises or housing cooperatives which currently own some 90,000 flats in the capital. The state generously subsidizes cooperative housing schemes just as the construction of family houses, while the city is obliged to provide necessary technical and transport facilities leading to the new sites.

Of no small importance for Prague's housing stock is the reconstruction of old residential districts and modernization of the old housing stock, ventures in which both the tenants themselves and local National Committees are involved. Back in 1960, only half the homes in Prague had their own bathrooms, in 1970 the number rose to 72 per cent, totalling 85 per cent in 1980. In 1960 a total of 54 per cent of all homes in Prague were connected to the municipal gas distribution system, in 1970 it was 71 per cent, while in 1980 76 per cent of all homes used gas. Similarly, in the year 1960, just 13 per cent of Prague homes had central heating, the respective numbers for 1970 and 1980 being 32 and 53 per cent.

Since the early 1980's, modernization of older homes has been part and parcel of state housing policy. Before the year 2000, comprehensive reconstruction and modernization of older residential areas are expected to prevail over housing projects on new building sites. In order to encourage and promote this desirable trend, Czechoslovakia has adopted strict legal measures to protect agricultural and particularly arable land surrounding Prague's built-up area. In spite of the great number of newly built flats, in spite of the demolition of old, inadequate flats and the reconstruction of substandard housing, Prague's historical centre and inner city still have more than 70,000 flats which require thorough renewal.

All over Prague, residential areas due for modernization are chosen stage by stage. One part of the district of Žižkov with some of the worst housing stock in the city is being completely rebuilt because mere modernization would be insufficient. But this venture is more or less

Since the early 1980's, housing construction in Prague has been giving priority to modernization and reconstruction. The former working class district of Žižkov, built at the turn of the 19th and 20th centuries, is now undergoing large-scale reconstruction. In the first stage more than 2,700 flats were pulled down and modern houses with some 1,900 flats are being built in their places.

an exception to the rule since older, usually multi-storey brick houses, and their services are still well worth saving and modernization projects invariably pay off.

Transition from new housing to modernization, however, is far from easy since substantial changes have to be effected not only in the planning and financing of such ventures but also in the building industry itself, its technical equipment and materials, in the qualification of skilled workers and last but not least in the evaluation of the profitability and labour efficiency of such projects.

Quite a specific task in this field is the regeneration of the historical centre and its architectural monuments. Particular care has to be taken to preserve their authentic image and often demanding restoration work, carried out by university-trained specialists, is involved. While reconstructing various historical buildings in Prague, valuable architectural discoveries have been made, uncovering for example priceless murals on ceilings, fragments of vaults and the like. In such cases, it is often difficult to return the renovated premises, often very spacious ones, for the purposes of housing.

In housing in present-day Czechoslovakia, both in new projects and rebuilding, maintenance and modernization, the order of the day is quality. This drive concerns not only the standards of flats themselves but also the overall quality of the living environment, its architecture and lay-out, public amenities and proximity of job opportunities and recreation facilities.

← *Vinohrady, built as a suburb in the late 19th century, is a typical example of the town-planning of that period. Almost two thirds of all flats in the district are due for renovation.*

Both new and old important public buildings stand side by side in the centre of Prague. The photo is of the neo-Renaissance National Museum from the last quarter of the 19th century, viewed from the Federal Assembly building.

3. PUBLIC AMENITIES

This term covers a whole range of social facilities serving the residents of the city in their everyday life. In Prague, naturally, these amenities serve not only Prague inhabitants but also people living in the Prague conurbation and visitors from all over Czechoslovakia and abroad. Some of them are of nationwide or even international significance. Public amenities include educational, scientific and research, cultural, medical and social-care institutions, commerce, public catering, communal services and administration. Some of these, such as Charles University, have a tradition going back several centuries, while others were founded only recently. All in all, they cover an area of more than 1,700 hectares and some minor facilities are housed in ground floors of houses and other buildings.

The education system which employs some 40,000 people in Prague, accounts for a broad range of facilities from pre-school institutions to universities. More than 46,000 pre-school age children attend the city's 450 kindergartens, over 130,000 schoolchildren go to its 230 basic schools; Prague has a total of 23 grammar schools, attended by some 12,000 students, 32 secondary vocational schools, 45 secondary apprentice training centres and 8 universities and colleges with 33 faculties where almost 45,000 undergraduates are studying. Basic schools provide lunches for more than 80 per cent of the pupils, the corresponding figure for secondary level schools is 60 per cent. Some 56 per cent of university students are accomodated in houses of residence and over 70 per cent take their meals in college dining halls. Most of Prague's kindergartens and scores of schools were built after World War II.

As regards universities in Prague, the College of Agriculture, the Faculty of Civil Engineering, Faculty of Architecture, Electrical Engineering and General Engineering of the Czech Technical University and Charles University's Faculty of Mathematics and Physics as well as the first stage of a university hospital compound in the district of Motol, have all been completed since the end of the Second World War. Prague's biggest houses of residence are to be found at Strahov, the local "student town," accommodating some 5,000 people and also offering a wide choice of sports facilities. The university houses of residence at Větrník provide accomodation for 3,000 undergraduates.

Public amenities in Prague include cultural, scientific and other institutions of nationwide and international importance. These are to be found in the city centre and residential quarters, with busy main streets forming centres of commercial and social life. In addition, large health and other institutions as well as universities are situated in compounds covering dozens of hectares each.

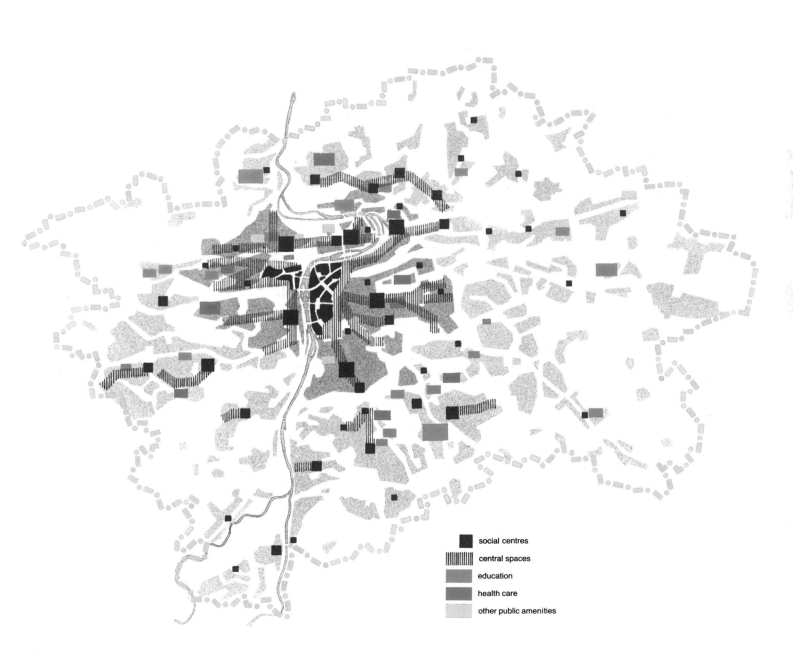

■ social centres

||||||| central spaces

■ education

■ health care

□ other public amenities

The Federal Assembly, Czechoslovakia's Parliament.

The headquarters of the Koospol foreign trade corporation, situated in the outkirts of Prague, near Ruzyně airport.

On the occasion of the centenary of the opening of Prague's National Theatre in 1983 its building underwent costly reconstruction. Three new buildings were added housing technical equipment, clubrooms and a restaurant and the Nová scéna (New Scene) theatre. The whole complex is noteworthy for contrasts between the neo-Renaissance style of the main National Theatre building and the modern steel-and-glass look of the adjoining buildings.

The entrance hall of the Nová scéna theatre features an impressive combination of glass and marble.

More than 36,000 people work in science and research in Prague which is the seat of the Czechoslovak Academy of Sciences and many other scientific and research institutions. The largest compound of the Academy research institutes is situated in Prague's North Town where still new institutions are being built.

Health care and medical services in Prague employ over 33,000 people. The city has 6 large hospitals, 14 smaller hospitals with a total of 10,000 beds, 33 outpatient clinics and many other specialized medical facilities. Prague's biggest health centre is the hospital complex in the district of Motol where a new paediatric university hospital for 640 patients was completed in the 1970's. Another hospital compound, offering more than 2,000 beds is under construction. The sphere of health care also comprises nursery schools catering for children up to the age of three. These facilities are situated in all residential districts.

As far as newly built medical facilities are concerned, special mention should be made of the Clinic of Plastic Surgery in Prague's 10th district, the Orthopaedic Clinic of the Bulovka Hospital or the Urological Clinic at Karlov. Since 1945 several new general hospitals have been built in the modern parts of the city. One of the first polyclinics was the one in the industrial district of Vysočany and in Břevnov, some of the latest additions are polyclinics in the North Town's district of Prosek or in the fast-growing Pankrác district in the southern part of Prague. The sphere of social care is closely associated with the health care system, the former operating many different facilities which mostly cater for senior citizens, children and adolescents.

The field of culture employs over 22,000 people, including professional artists, while thousands of amateurs pursue their hobby activities in their free time. Prague prides itself on 22 professional theatre companies whose performances are annually visited by 2.5 million spectators. Every year as many people view about 150 art exhibitions prepared by the Prague-based National Art Gallery, the Prague Art Gallery and the Central Bohemian Gallery. Furthermore, the Czech Fine Artists' Union annually organizes art exhibitions in its 12 exhibition halls. Every year, Prague's 18 museums are visited by more than 5 million people and its 90 cinemas are visited by 10 million. A quarter of a million music lovers annually attend some 380 concerts given by

The biggest single-building construction project in recent years is the Palace of Culture, opened in 1981. It houses two spacious halls, seating 2,800 and 1,200 spectators respectively, as well as a number of smaller halls, clubrooms and exhibition halls. The main hall, which houses a giant organ, has an adjustable stage and ceiling to improve acoustic conditions.

Most faculties of Prague's Charles University are located in modern buildings but the Carolinum remains the representative centre of Charles University. During its reconstruction, architects managed to harmonize the medieval architecture and preserved fragments of the Carolinum with its modern surroundings.

The Prague National Gallery exhibits its art collections in newly reconstructed premises. Collections of Czech Gothic, Renaissance and baroque art are on permanent display in St. George's Monastery at Prague Castle.

Of Prague's modern university campuses, the largest is the compound of the College of Agriculture for 1,700 undergraduates, including laboratories, workshops and student hostels well-equipped with cultural centres and sports facilities.

various symphony orchestras and other music ensembles and every year another million spectators come to see many other cultural programmes. In Prague's 560 cultural and community centres there are approximately 850 hobby circles, associating some 18,000 members. Millions of books are loaned every year to hundreds of thousands readers by the 740 public lending libraries in Prague.

The hub of Prague's cultural life is the Palace of Culture, opened to public in 1981. The Palace houses two congress halls, one seating 2,800 and the other 1,200 spectators, exhibition halls, clubrooms, restaurants and other premises. It is situated on an terrace overlooking the city centre. In the near future a new hotel will be erected near the Palace, forming a major architectural landmark as well as completing a congress and cultural centre near the Klement Gottwald Bridge.

On the occasion of the 100th anniversary of the Prague National Theatre in 1983 the theatre was reopened after thorough and costly reconstruction. Many visitors also flock to Hradčany Castle to admire the renovated Romanesque St. George's Monastery, housing collections of early Czech painting, or to the reconstructed early Gothic St. Agnes' Convent where 19th century Czech paintings from the collection of the National Art Gallery are on display. In addition to architecturally and historically unique premises, minor cultural facilities—such as cultural centres or public lending libraries—are built in new residential districts. An example to illustrate this trend is the community centre in the North Town's quarter of Ďáblice which houses two cinema halls, a house of culture with a spacious social hall, a shopping and a service centre.

The sphere of culture also comprises memorials, outdoor sculptures and memorial plaques as well as the protection and restoration of more than 2,000 listed monuments scattered all over Prague. Every year, over 200 million Czechoslovak crowns are earmarked for the preservation of monuments, with additional funds coming from institutions using these properties. The past decade, for instance, saw the reconstruction of Charles Bridge and St. Agnes' Convent, while Prague Castle and Vyšehrad Castle undergo permanent renovation; reconstruction work is now in full swing on the medieval market-hall, the Ungelt, near the Old Town Square.

This list of major cultural facilities, documenting Prague's rich cultural life as well as its educational, health care and other public amenities would, however, run to several pages.

Of particular importance for the life of the city is the field of shopping, public catering and accommodation with more than 10 per cent of all employed people. Prague has 16 department stores the largest of which are Kotva (The Anchor) and Máj (May). Besides department stores, the city has another 4,200 shops with a sales floor of over 330,000 square metres. There are some 1,000 small businesses providing essential services such as hairdressing salons, laundries, dry-cleaners, various repair services, rental and hire agencies, etc. In this respect, Prague is noted for its busy arcades, lined with shops and services. These passages were mostly built in the period between the two world wars but some of them date as far back as the Middle Ages. At present older arcades are being spruced up and the number of newly opened ones will be growing.

In all, Prague's restaurants, pubs and other catering facilities offer more than 100,000 table places and almost 60 hotels provide some 10,000 beds. Regrettably, even these capacities fall far short of the actual demand. Some of the city's best-known hotels are the Intercontinental, blending nicely with the historical buildings in the Old Town on the Vltava embankment or the new stylish Panorama Hotel, situated in the centre of the southern part of Prague. Many remarkable historical buildings have been converted into guest-rooms, such as the house known as "The Three Ostriches" in the Lesser Town near Charles Bridge.

The distribution of public amenities greatly affects the pattern of the city, its territorial composition and especially its social life. In fact, only large hospital and science and research compounds are situated in isolated, quiet areas, even though some of these facilities are also to be found in the inner parts of the city. Most public amenities, though, are concentrated in the busiest shopping areas in the centre, thus forming a network of community centres. Minor facilities, such as crèches, kindergartens, schools, health and shopping centres are understandably incorporated into residential areas.

Public amenities of nationwide importance, such as major cultural facilities, all the faculties of Charles University, art colleges, etc. are to be found—as we

Several specialized clinics of the Faculty Hospital in Prague have been opened in recent years, including the Clinic of Plastic Surgery, the Orthopaedic Clinic or the Urological Clinic at Karlov.

The Institute of Macromolecular Chemistry of the Czechoslovak Academy of Sciences was built in the mid-1960's in between the Petřiny residential district and the Hvězda enclosure.

The largest newly built hospital complex in Prague is the Faculty Hospital at Motol. The Faculty of Paediatrics, finished in the late 1970's, is complete with accomodation facilities for medical personnel. New wards for long-term patients are under construction.

The Intercontinental Hotel is
situated in the city centre not far
from the river.

Prague's biggest department store is
Kotva with a total sales area of
19,400 square metres, a restaurant
and underground car park.

said—in the centre and the main thoroughfares and squares are lined with first-class hotels, restaurants and places of amusement.

The inner city offers a relatively wide range of services which are clustered along the main roads connecting suburban districts with the city centre. A typical example is the district of Pankrác with plenty of space for shopping centres, whereas elsewhere costly reconstruction work is necessary. Newly built stations of the Metro are a novel feature in the network of public amenities.

Part and parcel of the social policy in Prague is the drive to locate public amenities of great importance in outer residential districts in a bid to broaden the offer of job opportunities and to enrich social life there.

A similar situation prevails in modern housing estates whose inhabitants still have to travel to the city centre for entertainment etc. In actual fact, some of the differences existing between the suburbs and the city centre in this respect will hardly ever be eliminated, even though cultural facilities in suburban parts are being steadily improved. Ideally, tracts of land should be set aside for these purposes and used according to social requirements and economic possibilities. People living in the suburbs will always enjoy certain advantages over inhabitants in the inner parts of the city in that they live in a better and healthier environment, closer to the country and recreation facilities.

Prague Castle is surrounded by gardens on all sides.

4. GREEN SPACES, SPORTS AND RECREATION

Nature and open spaces, such as gardens, parks and woods are an integral part of any city or town. Unlike some other cities, Prague enjoys a great variety and wealth of natural conditions.

In the past the relationship between greenery and built-up areas was determined primarily by social and technical considerations. First gardens were laid out near monasteries and later on near palaces. Larger vineyards and orchards used to be established beyond the town's perimetre. The most extensive of such areas was the King's Deer Park founded close to the Vltava river in the north-eastern district. The development of suburbs in the 19th century brought Prague's first public parks. It was in the year 1804 that the King's Deer Park was opened to the public and the first "people's park", nowadays known as the Chotek Park was built in 1833. As years went by an extensive green belt has been formed by the 56-hectare park in the Letná district on the left bank of the Vltava, the 86-hectare park on Petřín Hill, the Santoška Park in the district of Smíchov and extending up to the 20-hectare open spaces on the Strahov ridge and the parkland surrounding the Hvězda (Star) summer-house in Bílá Hora (The White Mountain), which spreads over an area of more than 160 hectares. Small parks are also to be found on the right bank of the Vltava river.

In several places the city extends up to outlying wooded areas which have been transformed into parklands. Such is the Kunratice Forest in the southern outskirts, which now serves as a major recreation area covering some 300 hectares, the 130-hectare Milíčov Forest bordering on the South Town or the 1,100-hectare parkland near the Klánovice Forest in the eastern part of the city. Transverse valleys formed by the tributaries of the Vltava especially in Prague's western parts, create romantic natural formations which have survived intact and are now protected by the state. First and foremost, these include the areas of the Šárka, Prokop and Daleje valleys, set in between Barrandov and the Southwest Town and the grottoes in the southwest parts, bordering on the Bohemian Karst protected landscape.

Prague's green areas also include gardens and orchards which—apart from growing vegetables and

Green spaces, sports grounds and recreation facilities cover roughly 10,000 hectares, i.e. over 20 per cent of the total territory of Prague. These include historical gardens and parks, forest parks in suburban areas and green belts lining transport routes or industrial districts. Not included in the total are green spaces and playgrounds in between blocks of flats, schools or gardens around family houses as well as agricultural land which is expected to account for one third of Prague's territory in the future too. The map shows a network of green areas, sports grounds and recreation facilities in the year 2000 when these are expected to take up as much as a quarter of the territory of Prague.

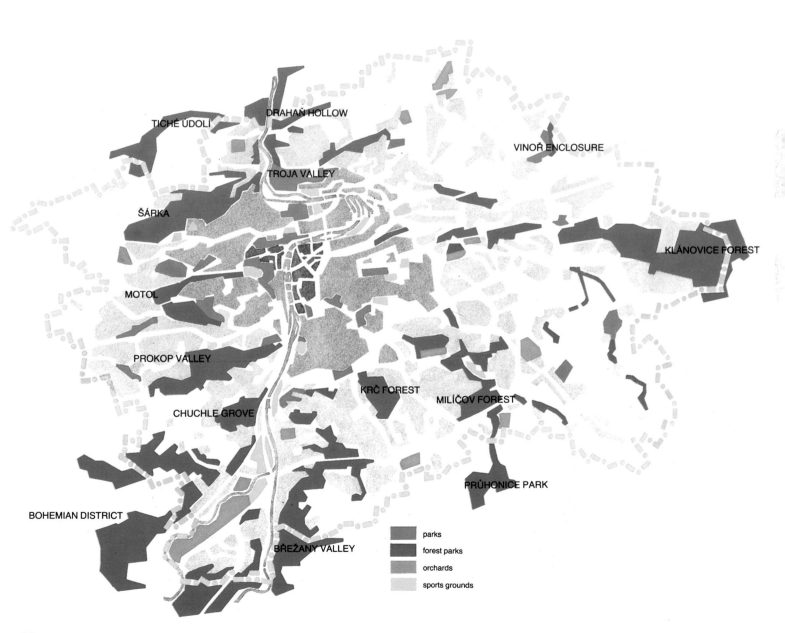

parks
forest parks
orchards
sports grounds

Prague is dotted with countless green spaces, including parks, orchards, historical gardens in the city centre as well as large parks on the outskirts.

Former gardens adjoining noblemen's palaces at Kampa in the Lesser Town have been connected and opened to the public.

84

The former Royal Enclosure, founded on the site of an ancient forest in the middle of the 16th century, is on the eastern outskirts of Prague. It is called Hvězda (Star) according to the ground plan of the summer house situated in the enclosure. The building, richly decorated by Renaissance stuccos, houses the Museum of Czech writer Alois Jirásek and painter Mikoláš Aleš. The whole area is opened to the public.

fruit—provide a welcome breathing space for Prague inhabitants and visitors alike. Many older garden allotments which used to stand closer to the city centre had to make way for housing construction and other projects. However, the total area covered by gardens has grown, thanks to newly laid out private garden plots. An average allotment in Prague covers between 200 and 300 square metres and owners are permitted to build a summer-house or shed, measuring a maximum of 16 squares metres and having its own cellar. These restrictions are imposed because no more agricultural land in and around Prague can be assigned for new gardens although there is a tremendous demand for new plots on the part of Prague inhabitants. In the past the authorities have permitted new garden allotments in areas originally set aside for other building purposes in the distant future as well as on tracts of uncultivated land. At present Prague has some 660 hectares of garden allotments which—broken down—represent a total of 5.5 square metres per capita. Added to this are some 430 hectares of orchards cultivated by the Parks, Forests and Gardening enterprise of the Prague State Farm.

All green areas, agricultural land not included, occupy 9,720 hectares, some 19 per cent of the city's territory. These include 968 hectares of parks, gardens and cemeteries, 5,226 hectares of combined parks and woods and 3,526 hectares of other open areas; the total would be much higher if front and back gardens of family houses in the suburbs were included.

The problem remains that parks and other recreations areas are unevenly distributed among the individual districts. Thickly populated residential areas usually have considerable shortage of green spaces but the problem has been somewhat eased by the current campaign to lay out small gardens between blocks of flats etc.

The maintenance and renewal of historical gardens and parks at Prague Castle is another major project in this field. This concerns not only trees, shrubs and flower-beds but also terraces and minor architectural works. Prague Castle parks and gardens form an attractive setting for promenade concerts and open-air theatre performances given there in the summer months.

The city's newly built residential quarters are designed in a way to provide between 14 and 19 square metres of green per inhabitant. Regrettably, open spaces in newly

In the 19th century most historical squares ceased to function as market-places and were rebuilt into public parks. One of the largest medieval market-places in Prague, Charles Square was also changed into a park.

The Šárka nature reserve on the northwestern outskirts of Prague, is known for its rugged terrain and special geological conditions. Archaeological finds confirm that it was the site of the biggest and earliest Slavonic stronghold in the territory of Prague.

The Vltava river is a major recreation area, its surface teeming with rowing, fishing or sailing boats.

finished housing estates are often completed only some time after most inhabitants move in. But experiences from Prague's older residential districts showed that after several years such green spaces are very beneficial, greatly improving the living environment.

Prague, as a city of more than one million inhabitants naturally needs adequate sports and recreation facilities. The tradition of sports and physical training in Czechoslovakia is very long, thanks to the existence of countless sports clubs, workers' sports unions and the history of mass gymnastic festivals and displays. This particular tradition is carried on by the Czechoslovak Spartakiads held once in five years in Prague's Strahov Stadium where as many as 14,000 gymnasts perform in one display in front of some 200,000 spectators. The Strahov Stadium is a giant sports compound, including a stadium for track and field events.

In addition to mass gymnastics and athletics events, there are many other popular sports in Czechoslovakia. Prague has several internationally known football clubs which have their grounds in different parts of the city: the team Dukla in the district of Dejvice, Sparta Prague at Letná, Bohemians and Slavia Prague both have their pitches in the district of Vršovice. Prague also boasts of a great number of facilities for track and field events, various ball games, swimming and ice-hockey. The multi-purpose sports hall in the Julius Fučík Park of Culture and Recreation houses a top-level ice-hockey rink. Another indoor ice-rink was built for the 1985 World Ice Hockey Championships close to the Hall. The recently built tennis compound on the Štvanice Island is an excellent sports centre.

Most of the facilities cater for top-level sportsmen, mostly Czechoslovak internationals, but the main task of municipal authorities is to promote sports and physical education on a mass scale. Hence, stadiums and gyms either attached to schools or built independently are scattered virtually all over Prague. There are more than 560 indoor halls, mostly well equipped for various types of indoor sports. In the summer months Prague offers a total of 1,100 outdoor fields whose number is steadily rising, as documented by the construction of a new sports compound, complete with an ice-rink and indoor swimming pool in the industrial district of Vysočany. Prague is expected to have more than ten square metres of sports grounds per one inhabitant.

As far as recreation facilities in →
Prague are concerned, new green spaces and water reservoirs, such as the Džbán swimming pool, are constructed.

The swimming stadium at Podolí →
offers one indoor pool, two heated outdoor pools, stands, a gym, a restaurant, clubrooms and other facilities.

The biggest sports complex in Prague is the Strahov Stadium. Since the 1920's several grounds have gradually been constructed, of which the largest has a capacity of 200,000 spectators and 14,000 gymnasts and serves Czechoslovakia's mass gymnastic festivals—Spartakiads. Another stadium for track and field events and ball games was finished in 1978.

After the end of the Second World War Prague had very few swimming pools. Nowadays the city has 15 modern indoor swimming pools and more pools are being built in new residential districts. The biggest facility in this respect is the swimming stadium at Podolí, completed in the first half of the 1960's. It has an indoor Olympic standard swimming pool with stands for 700 spectators plus changing rooms, a gym, a restaurant, clubrooms etc. Next to the main indoor pool are two outdoor 50-metre heated swimming pools and a children's pool.

The river Vltava, which used to be a major recreation and sports area in the summer months, now serves these purposes only in a very restricted way. The construction of a network of dams has caused a considerable drop in the water temperature in the summer. Therefore, 19 outdoor pools have been built in Prague, of which we should mention the Džbán complex in the north-western part of the city or the Hostivař reservoir, part of the recreation facilities serving South Town. A total of 48 boat-houses owned by rowing, speed-boat and yachting clubs dot the Vltava river banks, most of them near Vyšehrad. White water slalom enthusiasts can practise on the Čertovka stream, a narrow branch of the Vltava in the Lesser Quarter. Another water sports compound is to be found at Troja not far from halls of residence.

This area, bordering on the central parts of the city, prides itself on other major recreation facilities. An extensive botanical garden is under construction there while the nearby Zoological Garden, spreading over 64 hectars, is annually visited by more than 400,000 people and enjoys favourable conditions for further growth.

Prague's inhabitants have at their disposal sporting and recreation facilities not only inside the city itself but also in its immediate and more distant environs where various recreation centres, owned by sports clubs, industrial enterprises and institutions from Prague, are located and widely visited.

In present-day Czechoslovakia the prices of plots to build one's own weekend bungalow or the cost of an old house or cottage in the countryside are quite reasonable. The growing living standards have also been reflected in wide-spread construction of various types of recreational houses around Prague. More than 60,000 Prague families own a weekend bungalow or cottage

Prague has several indoor and outdoor ice-rinks for skating and ice-hockey. Skiers, as a rule, go to the mountains in the border areas but some skiing enthusiasts can try an artificial ski slope.

and on average 40 per cent of all Prague inhabitants leave the city at least three weekends a month. The greatest concentration of such facilities is near the Slapy dam on the Vltava, some 50 kilometres south of Prague. Whole new settlements of weekend bungalows have mushroomed in the area, completely changing the character of its landscape and resulting in some places in an overcrowding of recreation facilities. A positive aspect is that new green areas and trees are planted on previously bare tracts.

On the other hand, the regular weekend exodus of people from Prague is a sign that the citizens have a low opinion of the recreational attractiveness of the urban environment. Seen in this light, priority attention is devoted to the establishment of various "keep fit" areas, quiet areas and leisure-time centres in Prague.

← *The Troja Valley is a large recreation area covering some 700 hectares, including the Royal Enclosure, the Julius Fučík Park of Culture and Recreation, sports grounds, Prague Zoo and the newly established botanical garden.*

At present there are some 380,000 motor vehicles in Prague. This concentration of traffic poses a number of environmental and other problems.

5. TRANSPORT

The importance of transport in Prague has been rising in proportion to the development of its metropolitan structure, the growth of its population and its size. In 1937, less than 268 million people were transported by the city's public transport system, with one inhabitant using public transport 278 times a year. In 1948, the corresponding figures were almost 532 million people and 535 per capita journeys a year. In 1984, the number of journeys leaped to a staggering 1,200 million, which—broken down—means that on the average one inhabitant uses public transport roughly 1,000 times a year, or 2.7 times a day. The mounting demand on public transport is evidently caused by the fact that people now have more free time and have to travel longer distances from home to work.

Of considerable impact is the free use of public transport for children under 10, senior citizens over 70 and disabled persons. These advantages are also used for short journeys. Another feature of the policy is cheap fares and season-tickets offered to students as well as adults, the latter frequently receiving financial contributions to cover part of the costs of season-tickets from employers. Indeed, state-subsidized public transport is taken as a matter of course in Czechoslovakia. In an effort to curb the use of private cars for getting to work in the city centre, municipal authorities have been pursuing a purposeful policy towards this end.

Traditionally, the network of electric-driven trams which currently measures some 180 kilometres is the backbone of Prague's public transport system. Owing to its cost-effectiveness and clean operation it will be developed in the future and its routes will be extended to cover more than 200 kilometres. In 1980 trams transported some 35 per cent of all passengers. No smaller significance is attached to bus transport which operates on 800 kilometres of routes and carries almost 43 per cent of passengers.

The city's unprecedented upsurge in the past decades, its complex geological conditions, terrain and extensive historical centre were some of the reasons that led to the decision in the late 1960's to build an underground railway system, the Metro, with the perspective of becoming the most important means of public transport in Prague. In 1980, the Metro had 20 kilometres of lines, accounting for 22 per cent of Prague's total public

Antonín Zápotocký Bridge is another component of Prague's ring-road. The bridge has six lanes and a system of overpasses on both sides of the river.

Prague's public transport system comprises tram and bus routes and since the early 1970's the Metro. After the first section of Metro's B-line opens at the end of 1985 (A- and C-lines are already in operation), the Prague Metro will transport some 30 per cent of all passengers. In the year 2000 when the Metro will operate almost 60 kilometres of underground railway lines, it is expected to handle approximately 45 per cent of all public transport in Czechoslovakia's capital. Trams and buses will serve as supplementary transport means along with railways.

up to 1985

1985 — 2000

after 2000

Prague's road network, including tunnels and bridges, measures almost 2,000 kilometres. At present a new system of roads, made up of two ring-roads and 11 radial roads, is under construction. It is expected to handle over three quarters of all road traffic in Prague, considerably improving the environment. Some 150 kilometres of the basic road system will have been built in Prague by the year 2000 to divert car traffic from the central parts of Prague where pedestrian zones will be created.

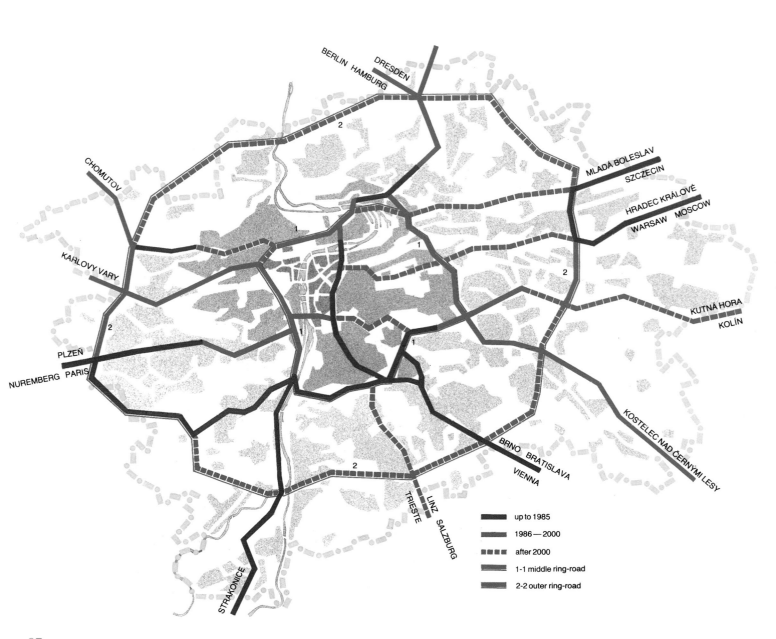

up to 1985

1986—2000

after 2000

1-1 middle ring-road

2-2 outer ring-road

← Klement Gottwald Bridge is part of the road artery leading through the city from north to south and linking on to the motorway network. The bridge spans the Nusle Valley at a height of 40 metres and is 500 metres long.

The Prague Metro is the most important means of public transport. Malostranská (Lesser Town) Station provides a graphic example of harmony between modern civil engineering and 17th century architecture.

100

Each Metro line and each station has its own characteristic look. The stations differ most in their vestibules, entrance and exit halls. One of the latest stations is Vltavská.

transport. In 1985, the Metro network was extended to 30 kilometres, carrying more than one third of all passengers. In the year 2000, the Prague Metro is expected to transport half of all passengers, while trams will account for 20 per cent, buses and other non-rail means for 30 per cent of passengers.

In the future, Prague must prepare itself for a further rise in car traffic. In 1956, there were no more than 23,000 passenger cars on the streets of Prague; in 1966 the number rose to 67,000, soaring to over 250,000 in 1983. Added to these are more than 38,000 vehicles owned and operated by public services and enterprises. There are some 26,000 lorries in the city.

The street network, in the city centre dating as far back as the Middle Ages, is protected as valuable evidence documenting the development of the town. As such it can hardly cope with the growing traffic demands. Therefore, a new urban motorways system is being built in order to protect the inner city from the adverse effects of car traffic and to divert traffic from the city. The system comprises an outer, central and inner ring-road and 10 radial roads connected with the nation-wide road network.

The length of the motorways system is approximately 240 kilometres of which almost 20 per cent of roads are already in service, including the huge Antonín Zápotocký Bridge in the southern sector of the central ring. By the year 2000, the system will be extended to 110 kilometres and will cover virtually all major directions, accounting for some 70 per cent of car traffic and substantially improving the living environment.

To solve the traffic problems besetting Prague is neither easy nor cheap; it is quite difficult to chart new routes bypassing the existing residential districts and public buildings. Furthermore, in some places antinoise barriers have to be erected and roads are built below street level wherever possible.

Given the varied terrain prevailing in the Czechoslovak capital, civil engineers have to build many bridges, tunnels, bypasses and flyovers. Thus, for example, to connect two sections of the central ring between the southwestern district of Smíchov and the district of Dejvice on the northwestern edge, a two-kilometre long six-lane tunnel had to be built beneath the Strahov Hill. Work started on the project in 1984. Another 1.5-kilometre tunnel has to be constructed in

A new hall offering direct access to the Metro and spacious parking facilities was built at the Main Railway Station in Prague in the 1970's.

The only Metro station so far which offers a direct view of the city is Gottwaldova Station, located at the southern end of Klement Gottwald Bridge.

the northern sector of the ring-road. The inner ring will comprise a car tunnel leading beneath the Vltava river. In some other sections this ring will include several fly-overs etc.

Parking space in Prague is yet another major problem. Today, 32 per cent off all cars are parked in garages, 11 per cent in car parks and other areas designated for such purposes and a whole 57 per cent of Prague's cars are parked in the streets. This causes some grave problems, particularly in the historical centre. The only alternative appears to be the construction of underground short-stay car parks, situated either above Metro stations, below flyovers or near public buildings. One such example is the car park at the Palace of Culture which offers over 900 underground parking spaces. In the evenings, the car park is used by visitors to the Palace, during the day by visitors to Prague who leave their cars behind and take the Metro. In the suburban parts of Prague, 8 cooperative-run multi-storey garages have been built, more are under construction. One of the disadvantages of subterrainean car parks is their higher cost and technological complexity, encountered especially in the historical centre and inner city.

Each Prague zone—the historical centre, inner city, outer development belt, industrial districts and recreation areas—is confronted with its own specific traffic problem. Some of the greatest difficulties arise in the central zone which invariably attracts the biggest crowds of people. There, public transport, and the Metro in particular, must be given top priority so as to create more space for pedestrians. Indeed, passenger cars are banned from crossing the historical centre, parking facilities are available only to local residents, capacities of public car parks are reduced and parking fees for longer periods are considerably higher.

Every effort is made to divert lorry traffic from the inner city and other residential areas. This is done by special ring-roads and the location of road haulage enterprises and transshipment depots on main road arteries in the outskirts of the city.

Inhabitants of satellite communities around Prague who commute to work or go shopping usually use not only the railway links but also the state-run coach transport system. Czechoslovakia has one of the world's densest network of coach lines. Every day, suburban

Prague's Main Station is a major railway juncture, which is to be linked up to all long-distance transport networks in Czechoslovakia.

buses transport as many as 127,000 passengers to Prague. These lines have terminals either in Prague's central bus station, near the city centre, or in several other places, generally close to Metro stations.

Railway stations and railway lines occupy a comparatively large area of Prague, a fact posing quite a problem to urban planners. The historical development of the railway system in Bohemia has made Prague a major railway juncture. The city has three mainline stations and three freight transport circuits. During the 19th century, the railway lines and stations were built in a totally uncoordinated manner. Considerable differences in their elevation make it extremely difficult to connect them into a single integrated network so that some railway facilities in the city centre could be converted for other uses.

Owing to the existence of the well-developed bus transport system, railways in Prague carry only some 114,000 urban passengers a day. In the future, this amount is expected to decline still further. In this field, railway freight transport is very significant as every year goods trains leave the city with almost 12 million tonnes of cargo, bringing in 25.5 million tonnes, including building materials.

Painstaking efforts are made to expand and modernize Prague railways as an integral part of the metropolitan transport system. These endeavours are reflected, for instance, in the newly built hall of Prague's mainline railway station (Praha hlavní nádraží), junctions near the Smíchov railway station, or the new station in the district of Holešovice. In all these projects, railway lines now link up with Prague's bus an tram networks.

As early as in 1937, Prague had its own airport, situated on the northwestern edge of the metropolitan area. For its time, the Prague Ruzyně airport was a very modern facility and since the end of World War II it has been extended to cope with the growth of both domestic and international flights. As far as their length and technical parameters are concerned, the runways can accommodate all types of contemporary aircraft. Its two air terminals are modernized in keeping with the latest demands on air travel.

The construction of motorways in Czechoslovakia, especially the Prague-Brno-Bratislava dual carriageway, has facilitated the development of express coach transport which has in turn replaced the short-distance

*The Prague Ruzyně international →
airport was built in 1937 and
expanded and modernized in the
late 1960's.*

The historical centre of Prague offers ample possibilities for establishing pedestrian zones. One such area is the street Na můstku at the lower end of Wenceslas Square.

Prague Castle is connected with the Lesser Town by the Castle Stairway. Lined by picturesque houses at the foot of Prague Castle, this is truly charming pedestrian zone.

air links to a certain extent. As to international flights, Prague airport handles on average of 2.2 million passengers a year. Compared with other international airports, this is rather a small amount but Prague airport has all the prerequisites for expansion.

Since the distant past the Vltava river has not only shaped the Prague landscape but also affected the growth of the city and constituted a major transport route. Centuries ago, rafts used to carry timber to Prague while ships sailed along the Vltava and the Elbe as far as the North Sea. In the 1950's and 1960's, five large river dams were built on the Vltava, a project that has rendered rafts obsolete, having improved shipping not only on the river but also on the Elbe up to North Bohemia. It has also set the stage for building vast recreation areas south of Prague.

At present, there are four weirs with locks and one simple weir on the Vltava in Prague. A new weir, complete with a lock chamber, soon to be completed in the southern part of Prague, will make it possible to increase the total of cargo shipped from the present 700,000 to 3 million tonnes a year. This will also play its part in reducing expenditure on road haulage and improving the environment.

Transport management in Prague is a truly complex problem, requiring both a long-term concept and massive investments. Current experiences show that not only the building of roads and other communications is involved, but that much depends on the relationship between residential and industrial areas, social centres and recreational zones, on the overall territorial and functional pattern of the city.

One of the three reliable sources of drinking water for Prague is the Želivka river reservoir situated more than 70 kilometres southeast of Prague. It supplies drinking water not only to Prague but also to many smaller towns along the line.

6. PUBLIC UTILITY SERVICES

In the past Prague could make do practically without any major public utility networks, except for water supplies, ensured since 1431 by the first waterworks in the Old Town. Water was supplied through wooden watermains to fountains scattered in the historical town. Remnants of the original wooden watermains, which used to conduct water most probably from the territory of what is today the district of Vinohrady, were unearthed during excavations for the first pedestrian subway at the crossroads of Wenceslas Square and Vodičkova and Jindřišská streets. Rain and sewage water was drained into the river through open street sewers. Prague's first recorded sewerage project was the drainage system at the Jesuit college Clementinum in the Old Town the construction of which began in 1638.

In 1854, the first steam waterworks, equipped with a filtering system, was built in Prague and in 1879 the inner town completed its first systematic sewerage system which filled in the gaps in the previous system. Prague's first sewage plant was put into operation in the district of Bubeneč in 1906. The year 1846 saw the inauguration of the first gasworks in Prague which supplied the town's street lighting system. Electricity has been used for these purposes since the late 19th century.

The growth of the city and its population necessitated the streamlining of the public utility services' supply and feed lines into unified networks. This was accelerated between the two world wars and after 1945 upgrading of the technical infrastructure figured as one of the key priorities. Today, Prague's public utility services include water supply, rain and sewage water drainage and purification, supplies of heat, gas and electricity, all kinds of communications as well as refuse disposal and incineration.

A particularly important role is played by water management which takes care of Prague's waterways, ensures supplies of drinking water as well as drainage and purification. At present, per capita water consumption in Prague exceeds 500 litres a day. This high amount is attributable not only to the population's growing living standards but also to considerable water consumption by industrial plants in and around Prague. For example, each of the two newly built meat-processing plants in Prague uses as much water as a town with a

Public utilities form a complex network safeguarding the supplies of drinking water, gas and electricity, heating, refuse disposal and sewage removal. Some of these networks, especially gas and electricity, are linked to the nationwide systems. In addition to their main function, public utility services are of considerable importance for environmental protection. This holds true of household heating in particular where the amount of high-grade fuels, such as natural gas, and electricity has been steadily rising.

water supply
sewerage
electricity supply
gas supply

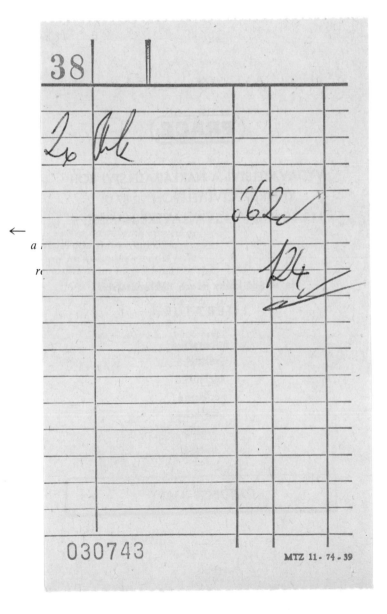

population of 60,000. Only a small portion of industrial enterprises have their own water supplies. The city's old water-supply system is also to be blamed for some of the losses.

There are three main sources of water supplies for Prague. The biggest of these is the Želivka reservoir which supplies more than 92 million cubic metres a year. The other two sources, supplying annually some 60 million cubic metres of water each, are located on the Jizera river, northeast of Prague, and on the Vltava in the southern part of Prague. One of the priorities is the reconstruction of Prague's watermains, a network which measures almost 3,000 kilometres.

Sewage and rain water drainage is another major problem. At present, some 90 per cent of households in Prague are connected to the municipal sewerage network. Only small communities in the outskirts, mostly made up of family houses, have their own local sewage plants or cesspools. The overall length of sewers in Prague exceeds 1,600 kilometres. In the central parts of the city sewers conduct both rain and sewage water, in the suburbs these are carried separately. After mechanical impurities are removed rain water is discharged into the nearest rivers. Part of the water, however, is used to offset changes in the water balance in areas with new housing construction.

The central sewage plant in Prague is located on the Troja island in the northern part of the city. Although this facility has been extended, a new one is to be built near the confluence of the Vltava and the Elbe. Beginning in the year 2000 or thereabouts, this new plant will serve not only Prague but also many other neighbouring towns within the conurbation and will also make it possible to restore Prague's Troja island to its original recreation purposes.

No one will dispute the fact that heating of residential areas is very important not only for the standard of housing but also for the living environment as a whole. Of all Prague households, some 30 per cent are heated by central heating plants, 23 per cent by boiler rooms and 47 per cent locally. The use of various fuels is also very significant from the environmental viewpoint. In 1973, coal and coking coal accounted for as much as 64 per cent of fuels used in heating, while in 1985 solid fuels made up only 30 per cent of the total. The use of heating oil has been declining, whereas the consumption of gas, particularly natural gas supplied to Czechoslovakia by the Soviet Union, has been rising. Between 1973 and 1985, natural gas consumption has more than tripled.

All modern housing estates in Prague are heated by central heating plants burning gas. Heating plants in the inner city and the historical centre are undergoing reconstruction. This is especially significant since the city centre is skirted by hills and industrial exhalations tend to linger above the city. An increasing rate of electricity generation will make it possible to heat particularly residential areas in Prague's historical centre where the advantages of cable transmission will be put to an especially good use.

As far as the heating of the outer residential quarters of Prague is concerned, hopes are pinned on the power-generating and heating plant in the Central Bohemian town of Mělník. Under construction is a 20-kilometre heat conduit to be completed in the 1990's. When operational it will help to eliminate all ineffective small-size heating plants in the northern and eastern outskirts of Prague.

The gas-distribution system is closely connected with heat supplies. In addition to the annual 500 million cubic metres of Soviet-supplied natural gas, every year Prague consumes some 380 million cubic metres of town gas, produced in the North Bohemian Brown Coal Basin. The distribution of both these gases through the nation-wide network is facilitated by 60 high-pressure and 220 medium-pressure regulating stations. In the coming years the number of households using the city's gas distribution system is expected to rise by 11 per cent and gradually the entire municipal network, currently over 1,500 kilometres long, will be converted to Soviet natural gas.

Another major subsystem of public utility services is electricty supply. Between 1980 and 1985, electricity consumption in Prague went up by 18 per cent, which represents more than 700 MW or 0.6 kW per inhabitant. The total length of the network of high-voltage cables is some 3.5 thousand kilometres. There are over 6 thousand kilometres of low-voltage cables.

Besides heating, industrial uses and household consumption, electricity is used for street lighting. Prague has no incadescent lighting and mercury-vapour lamps formerly used in the inner city have now been replaced by more efficient and energy-saving sodium-vapour

Small-size boiler houses burning natural gas are situated directly inside residential districts.

Water is purified and treated to comply with strict hygiene regulations. The water treatment plant is situated in the protected area surrounding the reservoir.

A waste water purification plant is located in the northern outskirts of Prague where the Vltava river leaves its territory.

In the 1970's, a new centre was built for Czechoslovak Television comprising editorial offices as well as studios and technical facilities. Situated in a park, the new television centre has enough scope for eventual expansion. ←

A new telecommunications building was built in the complex of the Czechoslovak Ministry of Communications in the eastern part of Prague in the late 1970's. ←

ones. Specially designed lamp-posts are installed in the historical centre of Prague to conform with the surrounding architecture. On festive occasions, Prague's major architectural monuments and important public buildings are ceremonially illuminated by floodlights.

As far as communication technology in concerned, two main tasks, namely the installation of telephones in every household and satisfactory TV reception even in densely built-up areas, have to be tackled. So far, some 65 per cent of households in Prague have their own telephones. There are 69 automatic switchboards and the overall length of telephone cables is around 5,300 kilometres. There are over 3,000 public telephone booths in the city.

Prague's fully automated telecommunications headquarters facilitates automatic inter-city and international telephone links. The two TV channels are transmitted in Prague by the Central Bohemian transmitter and a provisional municipal transmitter is located on top of the observation tower on Petřín Hill. By the end of 1994, a new television tower is to be erected in the district of Žižkov. This will contain a roof-top restaurant, commanding stunning views of the city's historical parts.

Perhaps every city in the world currently grapples with the problem of refuse disposal and Prague is certainly no exception. At present, the city must cope with some 400 kilogrammes of rubbish per inhabitant annually. Refuse in Prague is collected into 100 or 1,000-litre containers which are regularly emptied by a fleet of municipal garbage trucks. Special containers are set aside in the streets for the collection of scrap glass, while old textiles, paper and scrap metal is bought at scrapyards.

Prague has just one refuse incinerator, built between the two world wars, and this covers only some 20 per cent of the city's needs. A further 10 per cent of collected refuse is processed in a modern compost-making plant, the rest is distributed among several rubbish dumps. This state of affairs is, however, very unsatisfactory and work is already under way for the construction of another incinerator and a waste recycling plant with an annual capacity of over 300,000 tonnes of rubbish. The new facility will also supply heat into the municipal network.

The way to improve the performance, maintenance and reconstruction of all public utility networks is by the construction of underground conduits for all networks. This has been found to prolong their life-span and make it possible to carry out repairs or reconstruction without having to break up the road surface. So far, Prague has 16 kilometres of such conduits for the main power grid and approximately as many kilometres of conduits carrying all networks. The latter are found on several new housing estates. Work has already started on the construction of tunnels for public utility networks in the inner city, a venture which is likely to help improve the living environment in the city centre.

This brief outline of the city's public utility services concludes this chapter on the development of Prague. This chapter has perhaps made it quite clear that each of the above-mentioned areas—industries, housing, public amenities, green areas, sport and recreation, transport as well as public utility services—faces its own specific problems. Since these spheres are interdependent both in construction and the city's everyday life, town planners are known to dedicate considerable attention to their maximum coordination.

↖ *Illumination of the Prague National Theatre as well as other architectural monuments corroborates the fact that the Czechoslovak capital is also beautiful at night.*

← *Illumination of important public places is a major feature of night-time Prague. Street lighting in Wenceslas Square had to be refitted as the area was transformed into a pedestrian zone.*

THE FUTURE

Czechoslovakia's capital Prague has enjoyed over the centuries a long tradition of planned development. In the early 13th century the Havel Town was established as part of the Old Town and in the middle of that century a regular plan was drawn up for the Lesser Town. In 1348, Prague's medieval development was crowned with the grandiose layout of the New Town. For several hundred years the territory of medieval Prague, delineated by municipal ramparts, was sufficient for the purpose of the city. Nowadays, 600 years on, its large market-places and almost 30-metre wide streets still serve its inhabitants. New suburbs were built in 19th century Prague, particularly the district of Karlín with its classicist grid-plan or the district of Vinohrady whose characteristic features are a spectacular town centre and fan-shaped arrangement of main streets. The establishment of Greater Prague in 1918 made it possible to draft the first comprehensive master plan but unfortunately most of its ambitious intentions remained on paper owing to the prevailing social and economic situation.

When Czechoslovakia embarked on the road of building a socialist society after World War II, nothing stood in the way of Prague's planned development. The first physical planning document was drafted as early as in 1948 and systematic work on long-term prospects of urban development got under way in 1951. In the year 1964 the Czechoslovak government approved an overall master plan for Prague which, in fact, provided for the construction of its modern housing estates. The early 1970's marked another stage in the development of Prague, involving studies of the entire conurbation.

Since the early 1970's, the Communist Party of Czechoslovakia, the Czechoslovak government and the Prague Municipal National Committee have been granting special attention to the development of the Czechoslovak capital. Planners have since prepared a package of long-term plans, outlining the basic guidelines for the continued development of Prague. The "General Plan for the Development of the Capital City—Prague", as the document is officially known, represents a basic political-economic blueprint. In addition to this the government approved the main trends of the urban development of Prague, providing main guidelines for a new master plan which the government approved back in 1976 along with a regional plan for the conurbation.

The Prague territorial plan provides for the development of the city up to the year 2000, outlining long-term prospects in some main trends. It presupposes further development in the territory inside Prague's outer ring-road and comprehensive reconstruction of the older parts of the city. Special attention is devoted to green belts stretching from the city centre to its outskirts. According to the plan, the territory outside the outer ring-road will be reserved mostly for agricultural use or for the construction of family houses. In addition to the general territorial plan there are specific blueprints for individual quarters of the city.

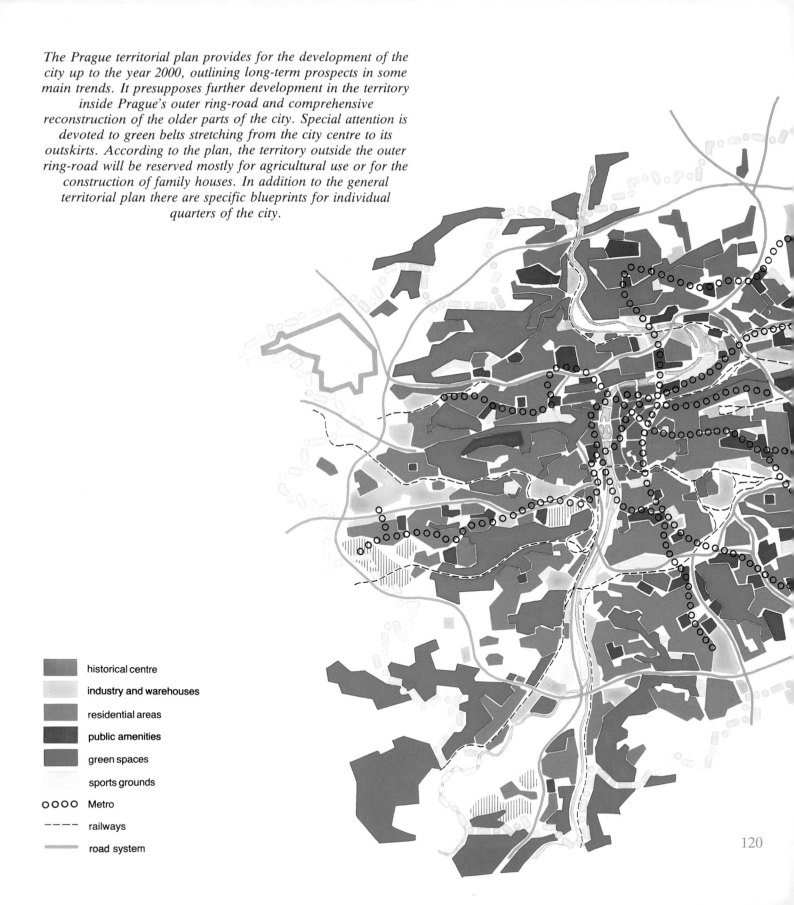

historical centre

industry and warehouses

residential areas

public amenities

green spaces

sports grounds

OOOO Metro

----- railways

road system

120

These documents formed the backbone of the subsequent detailed plans tackling the problems of individual areas of the city, namely industry, housing, public amenities, green spaces, sport and recreation, transport and public utilities. The authorities gave their seal of approval to the continuous construction of the Prague Metro and the city's road system as well as its water and energy supplies, sewerage and heating.

Since the early 1980's, there has been a vigorous drive throughout Czechoslovakia's economy to increase efficiency, cost-effectiveness and intensification, to economize with raw materials and energy, promote environmental protection and pursue a more coherent investment policy. The overall concept of Prague's urban development also has to take into consideration much stricter measures geared to protected agricultural land, modernize the existing housing stock and respond flexibly to changes in the demographic development of the city.

As a result of these newly arising circumstances and needs the basic conceptual documents pertaining to urban development, drafted in the early 1970's, had to be reassessed. Greater accent is now laid on environmental protection and a shift from extensive to intensive development trends. Unlike the former orientation on new housing construction, the order of the day now is maintenance, renewal, modernization and full utilization of the existing housing stock.

The overall concept is heavily influenced by demographic projections. According to these, up to the year 2000, the population of Prague is not expected to register any substantial rise. Its population, it is estimated, will be stabilized at the current level of 1.2 million. Naturally, this does not signify a zero growth rates in housing construction or other fields. The ever greater demands on the city's individual functions, the population's rising standards of living coupled with more stringent and systematically monitored environmental protection measures will inevitably call for further development and upgrading of the city.

Up to the year 2000, the main thrust will be concentrated in the outskirts of the city where some new residential districts are still under construction, but attention will be increasingly centred on the comprehensive renewal of Prague's inner city. This is crucial not only for a balanced development and for levelling out

The Southwest Town, a residential district for almost 150,000 people, will be the biggest housing construction project of the 1980's and 1990's not only in Prague but in the whole of Czechoslovakia.

Near the Southwest Town construction is planned of a new factory of the ČKD Tatra works well-known for tram manufacture. Thus the number of job opportunities in the close vicinity of residential areas will increase and a new community centre for the quickly developing the Southwest Town will be built on the land vacated by the old factory.

The construction of the Southwest Town coincides with the last stage of the construction of the western sector of Prague's South Town which will have a population of over 30,000.

differences in housing standards. In actual fact, continued growth of the city which already now sprawls to a great distance from the centre is very costly in terms of transport and public utilities.

Strict protection of agricultural land is also expected to have a marked effect on Prague's future development. Prague is surrounded by high-quality agricultural land and it is therefore expedient to assess future demands for new building sites much more carefully and critically. It is no longer desirable to encourage migration of inhabitants living in the central parts of the city to new residential areas for which fertile agricultural land would be needed.

The basic distribution of industries and other job opportunities in Prague is more or less stabilized both in the city centre and its industrial districts. In the future, planners will have to reconsider the concentration of work places in Prague's centre and devise measures to encourage the creation of new jobs close to modern housing estates in its outskirts.

Housing will remain a top priority. Up to the year 2000, the biggest building sites in Prague will be the Southwest Town, the western sector of the South Town, the Barrandov and Černý Most (Black Bridge) housing developments. To a considerable extent the improvement of general standards, including better environs and public amenities, which will be much more integrated than today, is bound to be projected in these residential areas. Family houses, to be concentrated on specially selected sites, will account for 10 per cent of the housing volume in Prague.

A novel feature will be intensive renewal of the inner city, including the modernization of houses, public amenities, and utility networks and regeneration of the historical centre. This is intended to improve the utilization of the existing housing stock, to check the trend of migration from the historical centre and inner city and subsequently to ease the demand for agricultural land. In order to encourage such trends of development, new building capacities will be needed, the structure of the building industry will be changed and the investment policy will be modified.

Housing and the location of residential districts is inextricably linked with public amenities and services. Apart from the construction of housing estates, complete with all amenities and services, another major task

← A new community centre is to be built near the Metro station "Družba" (Friendship) in the South Town. A similar centre is nearing completion at another Metro station "Kosmonautů".

← Apart from large-scale housing construction, many public buildings are under construction, including a new building for Czechoslovak Radio, situated in Pankrác Plain. This will be a high-rise structure which together with the nearby Panorama Hotel and the building of the Motokov foreign trade corporation is certain to become a dominating feature of Prague's skyline.

← The construction of the Prague Metro is continuing at a rapid pace. In the year 2000 the underground railway system is expected to reach 60 kilometres in length.

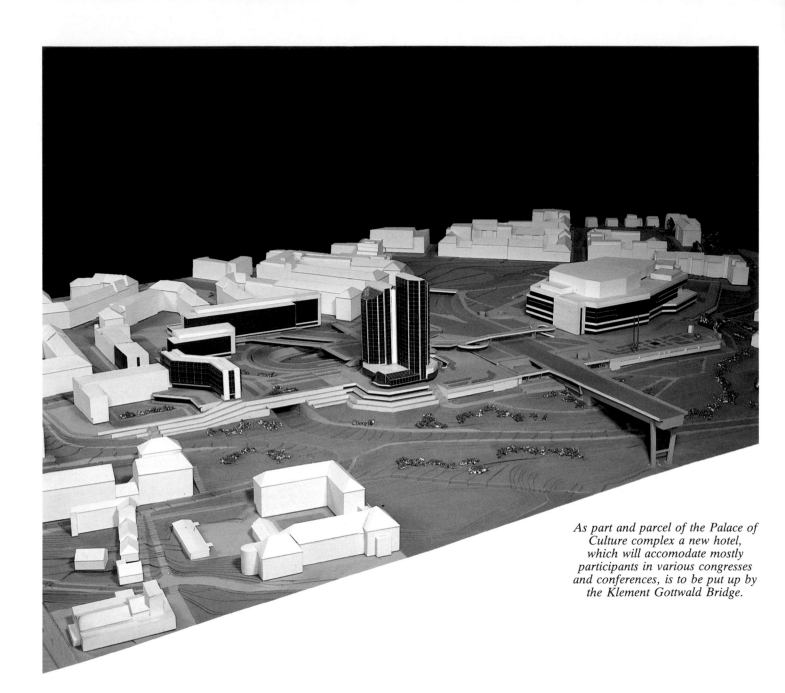

As part and parcel of the Palace of Culture complex a new hotel, which will accomodate mostly participants in various congresses and conferences, is to be put up by the Klement Gottwald Bridge.

Štvanice, one of Prague's islets, is a traditional lawn tennis centre. A new tennis compound, comprising training courts and other facilities, is currently under construction there.

Comprehensive renovation and modernization of older houses is the order of the day in Prague. One example is the district of Břevnov, situated west of Prague Castle.

Prague's historical centre is noted for its wealth of major
architectural monuments and important state and municipal
institutions. It is the hub of Prague's social life as well as the
main destination of countless Czechoslovak and foreign visitors.
The city centre, its construction and renovation, is a main town-
planning priority in Prague, aimed at preserving its existing
beauties and enriching it with new landmarks.

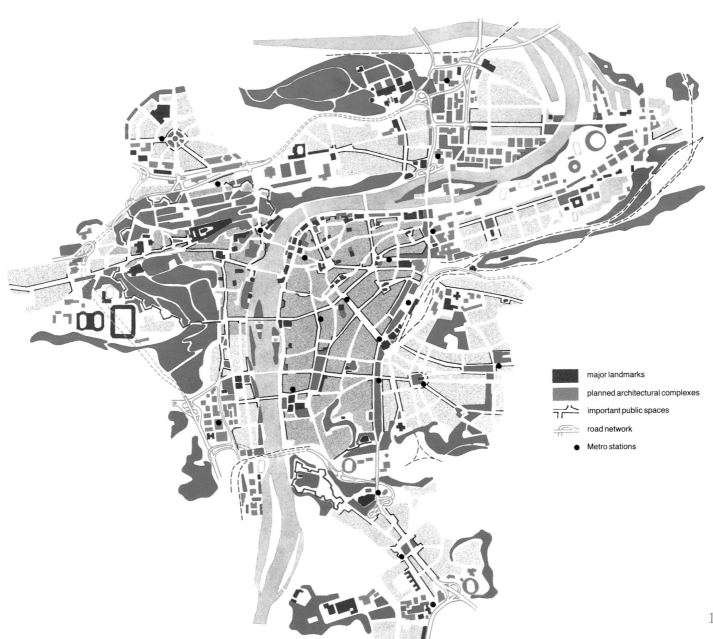

major landmarks

planned architectural complexes

important public spaces

road network

Metro stations

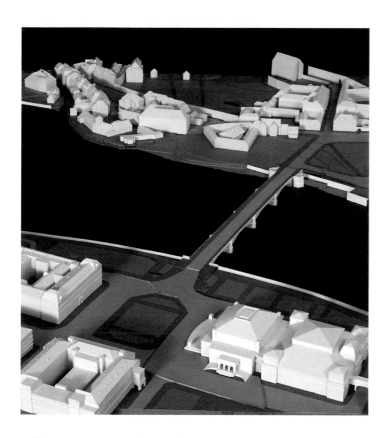

Every new construction project must be carefully assessed. Scale models (1:1,000) are used for these purposes.

will be the modernization of older houses. Under way are new types of integrated houses units which can be erected inside older built-up areas. Moreover, it is expected that ground floors of modernized and newly built blocks of flats in central Prague will house premises for various services etc. to a greater extent than today. In addition to local community centres, urban renewal will make it possible to erect—on a greater scale than at present—social centres serving whole districts and connected by public transport. On the other hand, public transport will provide better access to public amenities of higher quality, reducing the strain in the city centre. In the future, Prague will be enriched by some new major landmarks, such as new building for Czechoslovak Radio, the planned installation of the National Art Gallery's modern art collections in the renovated Veletržní Palác (Trade Fair Palace), the Palace of Youth etc. Other ventures will be the completion of the hospital compound in Motol, new university campuses etc.

In accordance with the growing living standards and the socialist way of life, sports and recreation centres and open spaces in Prague will assume yet greater significance. Thanks to its natural conditions and well-preserved parks and nature reserves, such as Troja valley, the Šárka and Prokop valleys or stretches along the Botič stream valley etc., Prague can look forward to new additions to its green belts.

As far as Prague transport is concerned, some of the main priorities are the further development of the Metro and the urban motorways system as well as faster reconstruction of Prague's railway network. Another problem to be tackled is that of car parking and the establishment of pedestrian zones. But the city's traffic problem does not boil down transport facilities alone but essentially depends on the overall pattern of the city. This means to provide better access between residential districts on the one hand and industrial, commercial and business areas on the other, between housing estates and social centres and last but not least between residential quarters and recreation zones.

The level of public utility services reflects both the growing standards of living and efforts necessary to promote environmental protection. In Prague this adds up to the following projects: to build up sources of water and raise its quality, develop sewerage networks and sewage plants, increase supplies of energy and switch over to pollution-free heating systems.

In the historical centre and inner city of Prague much depends on the reconstruction of the existing public utility networks if the current stock of flats is to be thoroughly modernized. Another task in hand are new public utilities, notably the sewerage system in many suburban communities recently incorporated into the city.

Environmental protection, too, is a hotly debated topic nowadays. A key document in this respect is the general environmental protection scheme including a package of measures to be adopted by municipal authorities as well as Ministries and institutions. The paramount goal is to reduce air, water and soil pollution and noise level. In fact, environmental protection in Prague has been a dominating theme in all walks of life, icluding efforts to raise the standards of urban concepts and architecture both as regards their functional use and aesthetic values.

Long-term development plans for Prague have been worked out for the period up to the year 2000, and in addition to that planners have outlined prospects up to the year 2030. The achievements of socialist construction in Czechoslovakia over the past forty years have convincingly demonstrated the viability of the socialist system, its ability to tackle major social, economic and cultural tasks. They also provide a good prerequisite for making the one-hundred spired capital of Czechoslovakia—Prague yet more attractive and beautiful in the future.

Jiří Hrůza—Blahomír Borovička
PRAGUE—A SOCIALIST CITY
Translation: Jan Valeška
Cover and graphic layout: Rostislav Vaněk
Maps drawn by Jaroslav Huml
Photographs: Jiří Doležal, Mirek Frank, Václav
Havlice, Oleg Homola, Petr Hron, Josef Husák,
Jan Jevický, Miroslav Kolář, Jaroslav Kučera,
Bohumil Landisch, Josef Molín, Dagmar
Nováková, Antonín Nový, František Přeučil, Milan
Racek, Jaromír Rajnoch, Josef Sekal, Ladislav
Sitenský, Dagmar Sýkorová, Zdeněk Voženílek,
Daniel Vrzák, Zdeněk Žáček, ČTK and Orbis
Press Agency archives
Editing completed in July 1985
Orbis Press Agency, Prague 1985